fast track»

STOCK MARKET INVESTING

KEN LITTLE

Publisher Mike Sanders
Acquisitions Editor Brandon Buechley
Managing Editor Jill Thomas
Senior Production Editor Jan Lynn Neal
Copy Editor Rick Kughen
Art Director William Thomas
Cover Designer Jessica Lee
Book Designer/Layout Ayanna Lacey
Proofreader Amy Schneider
Indexer Brad Herriman

First American Edition, 2022
Published in the United States by DK Publishing
6081 E. 82nd Street, Indianapolis, IN 46250

Published in the United States by Dorling Kindersley Limited.

Library of Congress Catalog Number: 2022934287
ISBN: 978-0-74406-180-2

DK books are available at special discounts when purchased
in bulk for sales promotions, premiums, fundraising,
or educational use. For details, contact:
SpecialSales@dk.com

Printed in the United States of America

For the curious
www.dk.com

To my family, a collection of writers, thinkers, and word nerds for providing their inspiration and love.

Contents

Introduction

Investing in the stock market can seem like venturing into a foreign country where the inhabitants speak a language you don't understand. People are shouting numbers and terms that are meaningless to you. Screens flash, letters and numbers scroll across endlessly, and it seems to be utter chaos.

Welcome to Wall Street.

The world you see on cable television and buzzing around the internet is only part of the picture. This part of Wall Street is dedicated to stock market traders, and every market move up is cause for celebration, and every move down is cause for alarm.

The other part of Wall Street is quiet, calm, and logical. It's where you find long-term investors who buy great companies at great prices and let them build wealth over time. When you become a resident of this world, you realize that about 98 percent of the daily noise surrounding stocks is meaningless to long-term investors.

This book is for long-term investors and describes how you can identify, analyze, and buy great companies at great prices. Long-term investors buy companies, so most of your work will be valuing companies, not stocks. If analyzing a business seems impossible, not to worry. Thanks to the internet, virtually everything you need to analyze companies is free or available for a small price.

Is it easy to pick great stocks? No, it is not, but it is also not impossibly hard either. It takes work, patience, and an understanding of the process, which is where this book comes in. I've boiled the process down to its essentials. When you understand the essentials, you are ready to begin. As you work through the process, you will gain confidence and learn more about the benefits of long-term investing.

Warren Buffett became a billionaire many times over by buying great companies at great prices and letting them make him rich over time. Will you make a billion dollars using this book's essentials? Probably not—however, if you do, remember who got you started. I do hope what you learn here helps you build an investment plan to reach your financial goals.

You might want to check out my website, investingforboomers .com, where I write about investing for retirement, especially for the baby boomer generation.

Acknowledgments

Many thanks to the fine folks at Alpha for all their hard work on this book: Brandon Buechley, Rick Kughen and Jan Lynn Neal. It is a much better book than what I submitted, and I am grateful for their suggestions, corrections, and general shepherding of this project.

Trademarks

All terms mentioned in this book that are known to be or are suspected of being trademarks or service marks have been appropriately capitalized. Alpha Books and Penguin Group (USA) Inc. cannot attest to the accuracy of this information. Use of a term in this book should not be regarded as affecting the validity of any trademark or service mark.

Chapter 1

The Basics

Investing in stocks can seem complicated and overwhelming. If you believe the hype, you might think that only a select few are capable of successfully investing in stocks. This is wrong thinking. Investing in stocks is not something you do without some preparation and some homework, but if you're willing to put in some effort, it can be a rewarding way to meet your financial goals. Indeed, owning stocks in some form may be the only way to meet your goals.

Let's begin with a brief overview of stocks and why you should consider using them to meet your financial goals. If you are familiar with stocks already, please don't skip this chapter; you may find that some of the things you believe about stocks are wrong. This chapter also serves to help you focus on what's really important.

What Is a Stock?

Common stocks, also known as equities, represent a unit of ownership in a publicly traded corporation. Each share of stock comes with certain rights, such as a vote at the annual meeting on important corporation matters. Because you are an owner of the corporation, it is important that you pay attention to the financial and market news concerning the company you own.

This book focuses on investing in individual stocks as one part of a complete investment program. Your investment program should consist of stocks, bonds, and cash. This focus on stocks will allow you the tools to identify great companies. But you can also own stocks through investment vehicles other than individual ownership. The most common ways are through mutual funds and exchange-traded funds. Many of you likely own both individual stocks and stocks through mutual funds or exchange-traded funds.

Although owning stocks through mutual funds and exchange-traded funds has some advantages, it is usually more expensive than buying individual stocks. However, many investors use several investment types to meet their goals.

Prices in Stock Markets

The stock market, or *markets*, as they are collectively known, price stocks continuously. These mostly electronic markets match buyers and sellers, theoretically creating an efficient process that prices equities correctly. Stock prices are determined by the daily market forces of supply and demand. However, a stock's price is strongly correlated to its value as an ongoing business. Even though other factors such as economic news may affect stock prices daily, the price will generally reflect how the market values the company.

Companies that show superior economic performance command the highest stock prices over the long term. However, the stock market is not always right. Clever investors spot undervalued (underpriced) companies and take advantage of the opportunity to buy with the hope that at some point, the markets will correctly value the stock, and the investor will profit.

Rights of Ownership

Common stock carries some rights and privileges that are important to individual investors. For example, you have a right to vote at the annual meeting either in person, by mail, or

electronically. Also, you have a right to bring issues before
the annual meeting that concern you about the company or
company policies. In truth, only large investors (usually mutual
funds, insurance companies, pension funds, and others that
own millions of shares) are really listened to at annual meetings,
although by law, every stockholder has certain undeniable rights
to bring issues before the meeting. However, if you own stock in
a company with an annual meeting nearby, I encourage you to
attend just to see how they are run. However, getting into the
meeting is usually not as simple as showing up, so investigate
what type of credentials you will need. The company will send
you a notification of the meeting called a proxy statement.
This document reveals the important votes at the annual
meeting. It also allows you to assign your vote to a proxy
who will vote in your place. The requirements to attend vary
depending on where the company is incorporated. If you
want to attend in person, the proxy statement will detail the
requirements. The proxy statement also contains important
information and is worth reading.

Some companies pay a portion of their profits to stockholders in
the form of dividends. While not all companies pay dividends,
those that do are often attractive investments, especially for
people who need current income, such as retirees. Many stocks
offer a dividend reinvestment option that enables you to buy
more shares of the stock with your dividends instead of receiving
cash. This is a great way to build your wealth if you don't need
the current income. Dividend reinvestment plans may differ in
how they work, so make certain you understand the details. I
cover how to use dividend reinvestment in Chapter 8.

The decision to pay a dividend and the amount is up to the
board of directors. Dividends are usually paid quarterly and may
be increased, decreased, or eliminated by the board of directors
as it sees fit.

Preferred stock is considered a special class of stock. Owners are
paid dividends before common stockholders and have preferred

rights to assets in the event of bankruptcy or liquidation. However, preferred stockholders can't vote at annual meetings.

Preferred stocks trade separately from common stock. However, the real value of owning preferred shares is that they receive preferential treatment for dividends. In fact, about the only reason to own preferred shares is for the dividend. For example, some industries, such as utilities, are known for paying consistent and strong dividends.

Why Invest in Stocks?

Historically, stocks have proven to be one of the most successful long-term investments that most people can make. The key phrase here is "long-term" because we all have experienced dramatic up-and-down swings in the stock market. If you want to invest in individual stocks, plan on holding them for a long period—at least five years.

Long-Term Growth Potential

Over the history of stocks, going back more than 90 years, investors have realized an average annual return of somewhere between 8 and 10 percent, depending on how the returns were calculated. That return is qualified with the understanding that it reflects the broad stock market, not individual stocks. Some individual stocks have failed miserably, and indeed, companies have gone bankrupt, which makes the stock worthless. Other companies have returned much more than the average to their investors.

The concept of buying stocks and holding them for a long period is known as "buy-and-hold" investing. Hotshots on the internet and in infomercials often deride this form of investing. However, it is a proven strategy that works if you pay attention to what's happening with the company and make adjustments as it changes over time. Buy-and-hold does not mean "buy and be stupid." If the company no longer reflects the superior economics that led you to buy it in the first place, it is probably time to sell and move on to something else. If you are paying attention, you'll probably notice the beginning of the decline and sell before the stock's price is dramatically affected.

Easy Buying and Selling

One of the most attractive features of owning individual stocks is that they are easy to buy and sell. Except for national holidays and weekends, the stock market creates a liquid market that will match buyers and sellers.

Being *liquid*, or *liquidity*, refers to the ease with which an investor can convert an asset to cash. Stocks, mutual funds, and bank CDs are liquid, while real estate is illiquid.

Because it is easy to buy and sell individual stocks, some investors are tempted into trading frequently to profit on price changes. While there are people who make money doing this, they are professional traders who, for the most part, spend a great deal of time watching prices on the stock market. For the casual trader who tries to time price changes by jumping in and out of the market, the result is almost always a significant loss of money.

Unlike some other investment opportunities, the liquidity of individual stocks means you can almost certainly sell your stock when you want to. However, there is no guarantee you will always get the price you want, especially if you have to sell because of a sudden change in your financial position or a sudden change with the company.

Stocks: An Important Part of an Investment Plan

Stocks are an important part of every investment plan. It is hard to imagine an investment strategy that could be successful over the long term without stocks as an essential part of the strategy.

Investors often combine stocks with bonds and cash to create a more balanced investment plan. Bonds, which are debt securities issued by government entities or corporations, frequently move in the opposite direction of stocks. If equities are generally up, it is common that bonds will decline in value. This relationship helps investors benefit no matter how the stock market moves. While bonds may provide balance to the volatility sometimes present in the stock market, it is the stocks that will provide the greatest return during the long term.

Buying the Business, Not the Stock

A significant part of this book is devoted to examining and analyzing businesses. This may come as a surprise to many new investors, who may have expected to be examining stocks. However, investors make money in the stock market by buying great companies, not great stocks.

Investing in stocks is really about investing in businesses. Don't be intimidated at the thought of analyzing businesses when balancing the checkbook is a struggle enough. The good news is that most of the heavy lifting when it comes to the number-crunching has already been done by people more qualified than you or me.

However, it is important that you understand the key metrics and how you can use them to make decisions about buying or selling a stock. You will put as much effort into deciding when to sell as you will in deciding when to buy. Chapter 3 will begin this process by identifying those sources that will help you in your investigations.

Relating a Company's Value to Stock Price

On a daily basis, the stock market can be extremely volatile, meaning there are big swings in prices, especially in those stocks that are frequently traded. The real value of a company is not necessarily reflected in the daily price fluctuations of its stock.

Frequent changes in economic data such as unemployment, economic growth, interest rates, and so on can cause stock prices to go up or down in reaction. While some of these changes can have a long-term impact on the value of the business, many factors that drive daily stock prices up or down have little long-term effect on the company's economic health.

Your job as an investor is to judge whether changes in economic or market conditions will have a long-term effect on the company's value. You don't have to be an economist to figure this out, but you do have to do your homework, which means keeping up-to-date with the major economic and market trends.

Buying Great Companies

There are a number of ways to define great companies. For example, some companies make tremendous products and feature glamorous advertisements that are very attractive to consumers. However, their financial health may not be the best. A common mistake in investing is to buy stock in a company you admire. While there's nothing wrong with investing in companies that you have an emotional connection with, it is important that you not let emotions cloud your judgment.

For the purposes of this book, great companies are organizations that consistently return value to their owners. In some cases, value can be the stock price that grows faster than the market in general. It can also be defined as companies that consistently pay a reasonable dividend.

These great companies will make up the core of your investing program. However, you can also find great companies that are defined by their potential. Frequently, companies like this are smaller but have exceptional growth potential. While they won't have a long history of financial success, you will be able to determine a value and assess their long-term growth potential.

Avoiding Greed and Fear

Two primary emotions spell trouble for stock market investors: greed and fear. Both of these emotions drive investors to make irrational and invariably wrong decisions. Greed becomes apparent when investors believe a stock or group of stocks is poised for rapid growth. If tech stocks are up, then you should be buying tech stocks. The problem with this thinking is that buying decisions are not grounded in any rational examination of the value of tech stocks, and market hysteria may have already driven the price up beyond any rational basis.

Some of us remember the tech boom and bust that saw stock prices rise dramatically beyond any sense of rational analysis. Greed drove prices higher and higher until even the most aggressive buyers realized they were not sustainable. When that happened, fear seized the market, and most investors sold their tech stocks for any price they could get. More recently, the real estate bubble that burst in 2008 and the resulting financial crisis almost destroyed our economy. Even though these examples may seem isolated, the same bad decisions that created the tech bubble and the real estate fiasco are made every day in the stock market. You can insulate yourself from many of these problems by investing based on a strategy that avoids fads and trends. You can avoid many of these mistakes by sticking with great companies that you monitor regularly.

You will know it is time to buy or sell rather than looking to the market to follow other investors whose buying and selling decisions may be driven more by greed or fear than rational thought.

Along with fear and greed, you need a good sense of the relationship between risk and reward. Chapter 2 discusses this relationship and how you can find the correct amount of risk relative to the potential reward that will help you reach your financial goals.

Taking the Long View

Investing in stocks can be an important strategy to reach your financial goals. If you buy great companies, you will find that holding them for the long term is a very rewarding strategy.

However, if you have a financial goal that must be met in fewer than five years, you'll need to find another investment vehicle besides stocks to reach that goal. Over a period shorter than five years, stocks can be very volatile, which places your short-term financial goals in jeopardy.

Investing for the Long Term

Your single most important financial goal is a retirement nest egg, and wisely investing in great companies will help you prepare for a financially secure retirement. As you approach retirement age, it is important to recognize the volatile nature of stocks over the short term and begin unwinding your stock positions into something more stable, such as cash or bonds. In Chapter 8, I talk about different portfolio mixes and how those change as you approach retirement.

Investing for the long term takes patience and a willingness to stand by your investment decisions even when others disagree. This confidence comes with experience and continuing education in recognizing great companies. If you have done your homework and are confident in your conclusion, don't be swayed by other opinions. Successful long-term investors continually review the companies they own to spot changes that may signal when it's time to move on. This diligence builds confidence that allows you to change your mind based on facts and research, not guesses or tips from others.

The Market Moves in Mysterious Ways

Long-term investors face a constant challenge from the stock market that seems, at times, to move randomly and unpredictably. In times of true economic crisis, you would expect the stock market to decline rapidly. This was certainly true during the 2008 financial crisis precipitated by a collapse of the housing and financial markets, among other factors.

When the market appears to be in free fall, it is tempting to do what many others are doing and dump all of your stocks in favor of cash or bonds. More often than not, that is exactly the wrong thing to do. If you still believe you own great companies, but it is difficult to watch share prices decline with the market, what should you do? The best strategy is to sit tight. Historically, investors who ride out dips in the market recover in a better position than those who flee a falling market and buy back into a rising market (sell low, buy high).

In 2020, the COVID-19 pandemic rattled the stock market as businesses shut down amid lockdowns and other measures. Investors holding a broadly diversified portfolio who held fast during this severe drop saw stock indexes reach new highs in the following months.

Fear of loss is a powerful emotion. If you invest in stocks, you will, at some time, suffer a loss. If the thought of losing money makes your stomach hurt, maybe investing in the stock market is not for you. If you can't learn from your loss and move on, stick with safer investments.

Long-term investors need courage to stick it out through the market's invariable rollercoaster rides. If you have done your homework, you will have the confidence to hold on to your great companies. By the way, market dips can be good times to add to your holdings at bargain prices.

Summary

Investing in individual stocks is really about investing in companies that offer the potential for long-term growth. That process defines the value of the business relative to the stock's price while avoiding emotional decisions driven by fear and greed. Owning a stock means you own a piece of the business, and your decision to buy or sell is not based on daily price changes but on the long-term value of the company as a business. Supply and demand drive daily stock prices. Your focus is the long-term health of the company, which may not be reflected in daily price swings. Individual stocks can help you achieve your financial goals but should be avoided for any need sooner than five years. There's risk associated with any investment, and you must find your comfort level with that risk. Owning great companies is the best way to improve your chances of reaching your financial goals.

Chapter 2

Establishing a Plan

Investing in stocks is an important part of achieving your
financial goals. The importance of planning for your financial
goals extends beyond the obvious and helps you choose the right
stock for each goal. The best chance for success comes from
matching investment strategies and financial products. Stocks are
one of many tools you can use, though the historical significance
of investing in a diversified stock portfolio suggests that you
may have a more difficult time achieving your goals without the
inclusion of stocks.

Investment Goals

Whether it's a retirement nest egg, college for the kids, a down
payment for a new house, or all the above, we all have financial
goals. You may have other financial goals beyond these. I hope
you have written these goals down in specific terms with dollar
amounts and dates for completion. Specific goals with specific
dates help you focus on achieving your plan. (For example, a
specific goal might be, "I want $50,000 in the college fund by
the time my daughter reaches 18.") More importantly, having
specific goals and dates helps you decide how stocks will help you
achieve the goals.

Major Financial Goals

Retirement planning is your most important financial goal because it involves the most money and needs the most time to achieve. If you are 25 years old, retirement is probably the last thing on your mind. However, if you are 50, a healthy retirement nest egg becomes a much more urgent concern. The irony is you might not worry about having a robust retirement fund at age 50 if you had started at age 25.

Regardless of your age, major financial goals are what shape the decisions you make about investing in the stock market. While a complete financial plan includes more than stocks, the other financial products you use will not likely make up the difference if you don't get that part right.

Timing of Your Goals

The two key parts of your investment plan are goals and anticipated completion dates. Investing in stocks for these goals is driven by both elements, though timing is the most important element. Stocks are your best chance for investing success over the long term. As I noted in Chapter 1, there are several ways to invest in stocks. I believe the case for using individual stocks as your primary investment tool (as opposed to mutual funds and exchange-traded funds) is solid with all the caveats noted in this book.

The use of individual stocks for long-term investing is well-founded, though short-term trading strategies (gambling, really) are not, as noted in the following sections. The record is clear that most people who try to time the market through short-term trading fail. What you want is a long-term strategy that gives you the best opportunity to achieve your financial goals.

The internet is full of businesses that want to do you a favor and give you the secrets of successful investing. Avoid get-rich-quick schemes that promise a way to quit your job after you make a killing in the market. There are no secrets to investing success except hard work and a long-term view.

When to Avoid Stocks

Investing in stocks is not always the best answer for a financial goal. There are times when you should use other products besides stocks. Investing in stocks to meet short-term goals is usually not a good idea. I recommend you do not use stocks for any goal that is fewer than five years from completion. Any financial goal you need to achieve in fewer than five years is exposed to a risk that the stock market will swing to the downside just when you need the money.

For example, if you have $30,000 saved for a down payment on a house and you anticipate buying within the next five years or sooner, move that money out of the stock market and into an investment that will secure your principal for the period. You can use a bank CD, a U.S. Treasury bond, or some other safe investment, so when it comes time for the down payment, you know the $30,000 will still be there. Stocks cannot provide that security. This example assumes you have made allowances for current and anticipated inflation, taxes, and other expenses. The point is that a volatile stock market can sabotage even the best plans over the short term.

You want to dial back your exposure to stocks and move into safer alternatives as you approach retirement. I'll talk more about this in Chapter 8.

Investment Strategy

Every investor needs an investment strategy; however, you don't need to be a Wall Street whiz to develop your own. It takes knowing how the basic strategies work, the appropriate stocks for that strategy, and an understanding of the risks and potential rewards of investing in stocks. Fortunately, we live in an age when access to important information about companies and stocks is literally at your fingertips. I'll cover how you can find the information you need to make these decisions in Chapter 3.

You can also find thousands of people on the internet who are glad to share their strategies with you (for free or not). Unfortunately, many of these strategies are really trading schemes that involve a lot of complicated maneuvers and sophisticated products (buying and selling options, for example). I doubt that many investors who buy into these plans understand the risks involved. Many well-meaning people (your brother-in-law, for example) who suggest an investment strategy for free may be great companions, but that does not qualify them as intelligent investment advisors. Some of these homegrown strategies may actually work, at least in some market conditions. Be careful accepting investment advice from anyone other than a qualified investment professional you have complete confidence in. A professional advisor will understand your goals and risk tolerance and only recommend investments that fit your individual situation. That's one reason I don't recommend an individual stock or any other financial product. Chapter 9 goes into detail on finding and qualifying an investment professional.

Your investment strategy helps you begin investing in stocks, and if you want to learn more (and you should), there are other books and many websites that you can use. This book is just the beginning of your investing education.

Your investment plan will use one or more of these three basic strategies:

- Growth investing
- Conservative investing
- Balanced investing

I cover the types of stocks used in these three strategies in Chapter 5.

Growth Strategy

A growth investing strategy seeks to grow your money (capital) over a long period. The goal is to identify stocks that will provide better than average capital gains (stock price appreciation). In other words, you are looking for growth stocks that can be bought at a reasonable price and with a level of risk that is appropriate for you.

Growth stocks, while potentially risky, may appreciate faster than the market as a whole and provide the best opportunity for significant long-term gains.

Growth investing can be riskier than other strategies. If you understand the risk associated with different types of growth stocks, you can set your own level of risk. There is much more about growth stocks and risk in Chapter 5.

Conservative Investing

As the name suggests, conservative investing is a safer approach to growing your money. A conservative strategy is focused more on protecting capital (not losing money) and less on growth. Each investor needs to determine exactly where their comfort level (or risk tolerance, if you prefer) is and formulate an investing strategy that accommodates those guidelines.

At some point, many investors will use a conservative investing strategy for all or most of their goals. A person nearing retirement is an obvious example. The need to preserve capital outweighs the need for growth. *Core stocks* may appeal to you for reasons outlined in Chapter 5. (In short, they represent solid, large companies that are the foundation of many investment strategies.)

Value stocks are underpriced market bargains to be sold when their true worth is reflected in the price per share. Value stocks, which I discuss in detail in Chapter 5, tend to be less volatile than growth stocks and may be a part of your conservative strategy.

Balanced Investing

Investors, depending on their age and risk tolerance, often choose an investment strategy that is a blend of growth and safety, called balanced investing. This investment strategy recognizes the need for growth to reach major financial goals while providing a degree of safety to offset the turbulence that can accompany growth investing.

A truly balanced investment strategy includes bonds or other fixed-income products and cash in appropriate proportions. However, because this book is about stocks, I'll stick to examining how investors can balance that portion of the investment formula.

Think of a balanced stock strategy as an engine that propels your investments toward your financial goals. Growth stocks act as the accelerator, while conservative stocks (core and value) are the brakes. As you change the mix between the accelerator and the brakes, you speed up (more growth stocks) or slow down (more conservative stocks) your progress. Also, as with a car, the faster you go (more growth stocks), the greater the chance for an accident, which is another way to say there's more risk. Likewise, if you stomp on the brakes (conservative stocks), you may not reach your destination.

That's as far as I want to go with the car analogy, but it illustrates how growth and conservative stocks work together. When you build a balanced investment strategy, you decide on the proper mix of growth and safety. As you grow older and have life-changing events (marriage, children, and so forth), you need to change the mix. Because life is never quite this simple, you will undoubtedly have several investment strategies for your major financial goals. After you understand the various strategies, the different types of stocks, and how they all fit together, you will be ready to shape your strategies.

Risk and Reward

Investing in stocks (or almost anything else) entails taking some risk. There is no investing in stocks without risk, and there is no real return without risk. That is absolutely the most important truth you need to understand when formulating an investment strategy. If you are averse to the idea of taking any amount of risk, then stocks are not for you. It will be more difficult (but not impossible) for you to reach your financial goals without investing in stocks.

One of the most important and often misunderstood considerations in shaping an investment strategy is the relationship of risk and potential reward in stock investing.

Understanding Risk

For a variety of reasons, risk is the potential for your investment to lose money. No one wants to lose money on an investment, but there's a good chance you will at some point if you invest in stocks. This is why your investment strategy must contain guidelines for buying and selling stocks. If you have done your homework, the time to sell a weak investment reveals itself before you have suffered a major loss.

The rule of thumb is "the higher the risk, the higher the potential return should be." You need to consider an addition to the rule so that it states the relationship more clearly: The higher the risk, the higher the potential return, and the less likely it will achieve a higher return.

Buying a stock that is risky doesn't mean you will lose money, and it doesn't mean it will achieve a 25 percent gain in one year. However, both outcomes are possible. How do you know what the risk is, and how do you determine what the potential reward (stock price gain) should be?

Financial websites report key ratios for stocks, and you can use that information to gauge how risky they are. While these scores change with time, they are a good starting point to help you understand and identify various types of risks.

Measuring Risk against Reward

When you evaluate stocks as potential investment candidates, you should come up with an idea of what the risks are and how much of a potential price gain would make the risks acceptable. Calculating risk and the potential reward is as much an art as science. Fortunately, there are a number of websites that have done much of the work for you, but you still need to understand the principle of risk and reward to make an educated investment decision as opposed to a guess.

The most common type of risk is the danger your investment will lose money. You can make investments other than stocks that guarantee you won't lose money, but you will give up most of the opportunity to earn a return in exchange. When you calculate the effects of inflation and the taxes you pay on the earnings, your investment may return very little in real growth.

Will I Achieve My Financial Goals?

The elements that determine whether you achieve your investment goals are the following:

- Amount invested
- Length of time invested
- Rate of return or growth
- Fees, taxes, and inflation

If you can't accept much risk in your investments, you will earn a lower return, as noted in the previous section. To compensate for the lower anticipated return, you must increase the amount invested and the length of time it is invested. Many investors find that a modest amount of risk in their portfolio is an acceptable way to increase the potential of achieving their financial goals. By diversifying their portfolio with investments of various degrees of risk, they hope to take advantage of a rising market and protect themselves from dramatic losses in a down market.

Minimize Risk—Maximize Reward

The most successful investment gives you the most return for the least amount of risk. Every investor needs to find their comfort level with risk and construct an investment strategy around that level. A portfolio that carries a significant degree of risk may have the potential for outstanding returns, but it also may fail dramatically.

Your comfort level with risk should pass the "good night's sleep" test, which means you should not worry about the amount of risk in your portfolio so much as to lose sleep over it.

There is no "right or wrong" amount of risk—it is a very personal decision for each investor. However, young investors can afford higher risk than older investors can because the young have more time to recover if disaster strikes. If you are five years away from retirement, you don't want to be taking extraordinary risks with your nest egg because you will have little time left to recover from a significant loss. Of course, a too-conservative approach may mean you don't achieve your financial goals.

Having Reasonable Expectations

Unreasonable expectations of how your portfolio should perform can lead to poor decisions, such as taking more risk to make up the difference between your expectations and reality. What is an unreasonable expectation? Expecting to gain 25 percent per year when the broader market is returning 8 percent is unreasonable. Expecting your portfolio not to fall when the market is down 35 percent is unreasonable.

What is a reasonable expectation of portfolio performance? As consultants are fond of saying, "it depends." If your stocks are more heavily weighted toward growth, it is not unreasonable to expect to do better than an index of the broader market that is also heavily weighted toward growth. For example, the Russell 1000 is a broad-based index of large growth stocks. If your portfolio is heavily weighted to large growth stocks, this index will provide a useful measure to judge your portfolio's performance. The sources I discuss in Chapter 3 have information on such indexes to help you determine what would be a reasonable expectation for your portfolio. This assumes, of course, that you built the portfolio with certain goals in mind and made your choices based on logical analysis.

When investors fall behind in reaching financial goals, the temptation is to become more aggressive, which leads to unreasonable expectations. If you choose more risky stocks (young technology companies, for example), you may have some winners that help make up lost ground, but the odds are higher that you simply fall farther behind. The stock market and the economy don't care about your goals or investment choices. The markets move due to a variety of factors and go up or down with no regard to your plans. When the market is rising, your portfolio should also rise (and perhaps a little faster), and when the market falls, your portfolio should not drop as far or as fast. That's the best you can hope for, and if you hit it, you are ahead of the game, as they say.

Types of Risk

There are two major types of stock market risks for investors: systematic and nonsystematic risks. It is important that you understand that your stocks may go down in price based on risks you have no control over. However, even though you don't have control of these risks, you can prepare for them and provide some protection for your portfolio.

A risk you do have control over is avoiding unwise investment decisions, such as not doing your homework, paying too much for stock, investing on a tip, and so on.

Systematic Risks

Systematic risks are those issues that affect the stock market and/or the economy. These types of risk generally hurt all types of stocks, although some stocks may be more susceptible to some risks than others are. Systematic risks include the following:

Economic risk. One of the most obvious risks of investing is that the economy can go bad. Following the market bust in 2000 and the terrorists' attacks in 2001, the economy settled into a sour spell. A combination of factors saw the market indexes lose significant percentages. It took years to return to levels close to pre-9/11 marks, only to have the bottom fall out again in 2008 and 2009 during the financial crisis. When the COVID-19 pandemic hit in 2020, the markets dropped sharply only to bounce back to record highs. Investors had no control over any of these events—either the busts or the booms.

Inflation risk. Inflation is a tax on everyone. It destroys value and creates recessions. Inflation is when too much money chases too few goods. The result is sharply rising prices that are not matched by increases in consumer income. This devalues money. Historically, stocks are a good hedge against inflation because companies can raise prices and pass them on to consumers. However, if consumers slow their buying, companies have too much inventory and begin closing manufacturing and retail facilities. The resulting slowing of the economy hurts company value, and stock prices decline. Often a recession follows periods of high inflation.

Market value risk. Market value risk refers to what happens when the market turns against or ignores your investment. It also happens when the market collapses—good and bad stocks suffer as investors stampede out of the market. Some investors view it as an opportunity to load up on great stocks at a time when the market isn't bidding up the price. On the other hand, it doesn't advance your cause to watch your investment flat-line month after month while other parts of the market are going up.

Geopolitical risk. We live in a global market. Political and economic changes in other countries can adversely affect U.S. markets. Most companies in the S&P 500 Index (the top 500 U.S. companies) have a substantial portion of their sales in countries other than the United States. This makes our stock market vulnerable to political or economic unrest with our global trading partners. During the COVID-19 pandemic, consumers became familiar with the term "supply chain." Lockdowns in China and other trading partners disrupted the manufacture and distribution of goods and components. Manufacturers rely on the supply chain to deliver components when they are needed. As a result, there were shortages and long waits for some items.

Nonsystematic Risks

Nonsystematic risks are those particular to a company or a small group of companies rather than the whole stock market. You can't protect yourself completely from these risks; however, considering the quality of management in your evaluation may help minimize the risks and as build a diversified portfolio. Examples of nonsystematic risks include the following:

Poor management decisions. Managing a business is a complex job, and the larger the business, the more complex decision-making becomes. A very real risk is that managers make poor decisions and those actions decrease the company's value. Most managers act in good faith and believe they are doing what is best for the company and its stockholders. However, managers sometimes just get it wrong and other times, act out of motives that are not in the best interest of the company or the stockholders. Spending time reviewing the key managers is an important part of evaluating a company.

Narrow sector factors. Sometimes an economic or market blip hits a narrow sector of stocks. An example of this is when years ago, the government imposed a steep tax on luxury items. Almost overnight, the luxury boat-building industry in the United States dipped dramatically. Another time during a domestic oil boom, the government imposed an excessive profits tax at the wellhead. You can imagine how that affected oil producers. Sometimes the problem is the result of unintended consequences. The market for inexpensive point-and-shoot digital cameras almost disappeared as more consumers buy smartphones, which all have built-in cameras.

You may not be able to avoid nonsystematic risks, but you can reduce their threat by doing your homework and taking care when evaluating companies. In addition to carefully evaluating individual companies, a diversified portfolio will protect you from nonsystematic risks.

If all of this seems overwhelming, take heart. Helpful websites and other resources offer much of the analysis you need to make informed decisions. This risk primer will help you better understand market risks and what to do about them.

Minimizing Risks

The best protection is a portfolio with the appropriate ratio of stocks, bonds, and cash. I'll focus on the stock portion of that equation. Some systematic and nonsystematic risks have no protection from the portfolio losses they cause. A major recession like the one that began in 2008 is probably going to hurt every stock you own. However, there are steps you can take to reduce or minimize losses from these risks.

Don't invest all of your capital in the same stock sectors, and diversify by size. Own some (not more than 10 percent) foreign stocks to help offset problems caused in the domestic economy. I discuss building portfolios that vary from aggressive to conservative in Chapter 8. These strategies will help you avoid some of the market risks facing all stock investors.

The Traps of Trading– Your Biggest Risk

Market timing may be the two most dangerous words in investing, especially when practiced by beginners. Market timing is attempting to predict future price movements through the use of various technical analysis tools. At its best, market timing is a risky business for professional investors. The real danger exists for beginners who are tempted by what looks like easy money. All you have to do is buy a stock today and sell it tomorrow on a "gut feeling it was going up." Yes, this happens every once in a while, because somebody has to win the lottery, too. (Here's a hint: It won't be you or me.)

Professional traders use highly sophisticated trading techniques driven by computer programs that analyze huge volumes of data almost instantly. You are competing with them when you attempt to play the trading game, and you will probably lose. Professional traders have a name for amateurs who believe they can win: "dumb money." With all of their technology and huge bankrolls behind them, not even all professional traders are successful for an extended period.

Summary

Plan for your financial goals and you increase the odds of success. Your plan suits your goals, resources, time frame, and tolerance for risks. Your investment strategy executes the steps needed to meet your financial goals. You face risk in any investment strategy, and understanding the different types of risk helps you craft a plan that works best for you. Some amount of risk is unavoidable and out of your control. Other types of risk can be mitigated with your investment strategy. Trading for short-term gains is the riskiest action you can take and should be absolutely avoided.

Chapter 3

Finding and Understanding Information

The internet is the best and worst source of reliable financial information. No other resource offers you the depth and breadth of information that is available virtually instantly and often at no cost to you.

However, the internet is like those cheesy "evil twin" movie plots where a character is split into its good side and its evil side. Because they look exactly alike, how do you tell the good one from its evil twin?

On reliable websites, you can find the same information in documents from the regulatory reports that companies must file. Reliable websites digest and organize the information, so it's actually useful. These sites may add analysis and commentary along with news stories that impact the markets and the economy.

The underside of the internet is little more than a slick way to separate you and your money. Some may present themselves as legitimate news organizations, but it doesn't take long to figure out there's an agenda of promotion underlying most of the content. Other sites promise nonsense such as "the billionaire's secret" for turning your $10,000 into $10 million. There will be "testimonials" from satisfied customers describing life-changing gains. Others hint they have special insights or information not available to the general public that will return ten times your investment. While websites still promote scams and schemes, social media has taken the lead in suckering people into a funnel of deception. Here's a simple rule: Never invest in anything promoted on social media, including forums, lists, chat rooms, and so on. I could write a whole book on the various scams, cons, and frauds I've seen over 25-plus years of covering investing and personal finance.

Where to Find Reliable Information

There are a number of websites that do offer reliable information and news that investors can use. The best take the regulatory filings all publicly traded companies must make and compute financial ratios and other metrics. Equally important, you can compare companies with peers and market indexes. You can analyze companies to a degree that would've been impossible before the internet without spending hours poring over documents and doing your own calculations.

The real problem is not a lack of information, but too much information for many people. Sorting through all the websites that offer company information, or even one website, can be confusing and disheartening unless you know what to look for. One of the most important tools investors need to master is the stock screen, which will help identify companies worthy of more research. More on stock screens later in this chapter.

Finding Information on the Internet

Finding information on the internet is easy if you know where to look and where not to look. Clearly, some resources are better than others for information on specific companies. For many people, Google or another search engine is an obvious starting point. The problem with using search engines such as Google is that you get too much information, and the websites ranked near the top might not be good resources. However, search engines can be helpful if you are looking for a specific answer, such as: What were IBM's earnings last quarter?

Although search engines can be helpful, you will save time by going directly to key information sources.

I have several suggestions for reputable sources that offer tools to help you manage information, as well as find it. I also have some suggestions about avoiding content that is biased and seeks to promote a particular product, such as a stock-picking service. Later in this chapter, I introduce you to stock screens. If you are not already a user of these helpful assistants, you are in for a pleasant surprise.

Morningstar

Morningstar (morningstar.com) is one of the best sources of company news and information on the internet, as far as I'm concerned. The site has a free section and a paid subscription area that contains much more detailed information and tools. However, the free section has enough information for many investors to find all they need to know. Morningstar made its reputation by providing detailed and comprehensive information on mutual funds. Later they expanded to include stocks and other securities.

Over the years, I have used both the free and paid sections. The free section has all the information you need to help you make good stock decisions. The subscription area has richer detail and comprehensive portfolio management tools. Two features stand out in my experience: the premium screen tool and the in-depth analysis. The subscription covers all of the securities Morningstar follows in addition to stocks. If you want to drill deeper, the subscription is well worth the money. Morningstar offers a free trial if you want to explore their more detailed information and recommendations. If you anticipate investing a large sum, the paid subscription is well worth the price. However, the free resources are comprehensive and deep enough for many investors.

One of the rich features is historical data for many for the financial ratios and other metrics. This lets you see trends over long periods. How a company performs in all types of market conditions (rising or falling) and economic cycles (boom or bust) tells you what you might expect when these conditions return. An interactive chart feature lets you set different looks and compare the stock to market indexes and/or other stocks. There's more information on stock indexes and their importance later in this chapter.

Yahoo! Finance

Yahoo! Finance (www.finance.yahoo.com) is a treasure chest of information on companies and stocks—along with other securities. What it lacks in design, it makes up for in rich content features, including economic, market, company features, and other investing news.

One feature that stands out is their historical price database. This allows you to look back at stock prices by day or month and lets you select a date range. Using this feature, you can watch a stock's performance during the period. How did the stock's price hold up during market volatility or when there were major turns in the economy? You can download the information and open it in a program such as Microsoft Excel for further analysis.

The website reports analysts' opinions, but rather than give you the full report (some of which are available for purchase from the individual analysts), it offers a summary of their findings.

Price Target

The price target is a share price analysts say the stock will achieve at some future date. Analysts often attach a period to the price, such as a one-year price target of $19. The information is more suggestive than quantifiable. It is helpful for getting a sense of what others are thinking about the stock's price.

For example, here is a table showing how analysts ranked one company:

Price Target	Summary
Mean target	21.71
Median target	21
High target	25
Low target	19
Number of brokers	14

At a glance, you can see that the 14 analysts that follow this stock have different opinions on the *price target* or the price they believe is appropriate for this particular stock. The consensus is around $21 per share; however, at least one felt it should be $25, while another saw it at $19. This difference of opinion is typical. At the time this information was gathered, the stock had closed the day before at $19.24 per share. Analysts rate companies as one of two major recommendations— "buy" or "sell"—although they may use "hold" as a neutral recommendation. Some add superlatives, but another way is to use a scale that ranges from strong buy to strong sell. Here is an example from Yahoo! Finance:

Recommendation Summary*

Mean Recommendation (this week):   1.9

Mean Recommendation (last week):   1.9

Change: 0.0

*(Strong Buy) 1.0—5.0 (Sell)

This scale tells you that most analysts still feel enthusiastic about this stock and that sentiment hasn't changed from last week.

Yahoo! Finance also has a strong charting feature, which is handy for those who prefer a visual reference to numbers. You can track stocks (or stock indexes) and compare companies in the same industry on the same chart, along with a base index.

A note of caution: Yahoo! Finance includes sponsored content, meaning the article was submitted by someone promoting a product or service. Sponsored articles are noted with a small note above the headline, such as "Ad (company name)" or "Sponsored content." These "articles" are advertisements and should be avoided in most cases.

Investopedia

Investopedia (investopedia.com) is a gold mine of information on investing terms and concepts. If you run across investing terms or concepts, this is the place to go for reliable information. They also offer the usual charts and data on stocks and other investing opportunities. One of the unusual features is the Stock Market Simulator that lets you practice investing without risking any real money.

Other Resource Websites

Following are several other websites I turn to for information, although I use these less frequently than Morningstar or Yahoo! Finance. You may have other favorites you find helpful.

MSN.money. Microsoft Money (money.msn.com) offers many helpful tools for investing in individual stocks. In addition to comprehensive news coverage of stocks and the stock market, the site has some useful analytical tools. The site allows you to build your own watch list and follow your own group of stocks. You can find this feature on many other websites. Like other sites, Microsoft Money links to other websites for much of the news content. It also contains sponsored content that is marked with an "ad" icon.

MarketWatch. This site (marketwatch.com) provides comprehensive news and information as well as several key features for stock investors. The website rates stocks using a number of factors and is fond of lists. This is a subscription website, but you can look around without subscribing for a limited time. If you want access to news and analysis, MarketWatch is worth the subscription. MarketWatch and Barron's (a robust news site) share content.

Here are some other websites to consider. Most require a subscription to enjoy the more robust features and virtually all intersperse ads with regular content, so be wary of what you click.

Forbes. Forbes is the website (forbes.com) of the venerable business magazine and has the comprehensive news coverage you would expect. It is a good resource to stay on top of company news as well as important information on changes in the economy.

The Wall Street Journal. Considered the bible of business news, WSJ.com carries on the tradition of the famous newspaper.

Bloomberg. Bloomberg.com covers a broad range of business, investing, personal finance, and lifestyle news. The business was built on providing quick news to investment professionals before there was an internet. You'll find plenty of news and opinion, but not much in the way of investing tools unless you subscribe to their service.

This is by no means a comprehensive list, and if you use your critical thinking skills, you can find other legitimate sources.

Information You Should Avoid

Information on the internet ranges from incredibly useful to outright fraud. Your best bet is to stick with the websites I've previously mentioned or other mainstream sources of information. Here are some tips on information you should avoid:

- Any suggestion that you should invest in penny stocks. *Penny stocks* are not listed on any major stock exchange and trade for a few dollars a share or less. The companies are very small and have a low long-term survival rate. There is nothing wrong with most of the companies; however, penny stocks are often used in scams.

- Any unsolicited advice you receive by email, even if it appears to be someone you know.

- Avoid any links that purport to connect you with "investor secrets revealed," "Wall Street insider information," "millionaire investor shares secrets," or any other plan that promises easy riches in the stock market.

- Don't visit chat rooms or forums, even on well-known websites.

There are no secrets to investing success. There is only work and a plan that fits your financial goals and tolerance for risk.

Which Numbers Are Important?

For the long-term investor, picking stocks is about understanding the important numbers. Long-term investors are not concerned with daily price fluctuations in a stock, because they are buying a company, and it is the company's fundamental financial health that is important.

The value of a stock is directly related to the value of the business and is primarily concerned with earnings. The purpose of a business is to make money for its owners, and the more profitable a company is, the more valuable it is to its owners and others who want to own shares. In Chapter 6, I talk about the difference between stock value and stock price. It is easy to find historical information about a company's profits, but that is only part of the picture.

Stockholders are most interested in future profits, and historical information is not predictive of future results. A company with a lengthy history of earning consistent profits is most likely to continue that trend; however, there are no guarantees that it will.

Your job as a long-term investor is to identify companies that meet your financial goals with an acceptable amount of risk. The selection process involves a certain amount of looking into the future and using those projections to establish the fair value for the stock today. In upcoming chapters, I help you understand how to arrive at that value using several tools in different types of analysis. I'll start with the company's financial statements, which are covered in Chapter 4.

Understanding Indexes and Their Importance

It's important to monitor how well your stocks are doing. You can see if the price is up or down, but how does that compare to the overall market? One way is to use stock indexes as a relative measuring tool. Stock indexes are continuously updated during trading hours and show investor sentiment in real-time. If the stock market is rising based on an index, how is my stock comparing? I discuss stock screens in the next section and how to use indexes to compare performance. The three major stock indexes are:

- The Standard & Poor's 500 tracks 500 of the largest companies and represents about 80 percent of the total stock market value. Professional investors consider the S&P 500 most representative of the total market.

- The Dow Jones Industrial Average often gets more popular press attention, although it only represents 30 large and influential companies. The Dow is often seen as an indicator of expectations.

- The Nasdaq Composite is best known for its heavy representation of technology stocks, although there are stocks in many other sectors. The Nasdaq contains companies of all sizes and some that are more speculative in nature.

There are literally thousands of indexes, but these three are generally all you'll need. If you want to get into the weeds of how the indexes work, there are plenty of resources on the internet. Investopedia is a good place to start.

However, before diving into the deep pool of a financial analysis, you need a way to begin the selection process by narrowing down a list of possible investment candidates to a manageable level. The best tool for this job is the stock screen.

How to Use a Stock Screen

A *stock screen* is a tool offered on many websites, including those mentioned in this chapter, that helps investors sort through thousands of available stocks. Stock screens filter the list based on criteria you select and deliver a list of stocks that you can filter further or begin researching in depth. A good stock screen saves you time and helps you focus on potential investment candidates.

Stock screens range from fairly simple to quite complex. The more complex the screen, the more details it will filter for you. As you get started with screens, stick to the simpler ones and then move on to the more complicated screens. Many basic stock screens have presets that have already done the work of selecting the criteria for you. They can be helpful, especially when starting out in understanding how screens work; just be certain you understand what criteria the screen is using so the results are meaningful. If it helps, think of a stock screen as a search engine for stocks.

The Best Stock Screen

I use Morningstar's stock screen the most. The version on the free portion of the website is very robust and delivers excellent results. The screen in the paid area is more detailed and will take some time to master.

I like Morningstar's (free) screen for two important reasons. First, Morningstar uses some proprietary measurements on its website and on its screen. For example, they assign a grade for growth, profitability, and financial health. Morningstar also places every stock into a nine-square grid called a style box. The style box uses growth, core, and value across the top and large, mid, or small along the side. This puts every stock into a square based on its size and type.

All of the proprietary measurements, along with traditional metrics, are defined throughout the site. For example, in the stock screen, each criterion has a light bulb icon next to its name. When you click on the light bulb, a window opens with the definition or explanation of the variable.

The task of mastering the stock screen tool is the most important objective in the early stages of learning about investing in stocks. Whether you use Morningstar's or another, a good knowledge of the stock screen is vital to your success. As you work through this book, you'll build an understanding of the terms used in screens and which are the most important for your personal search.

Using Morningstar's Stock Screen

The first tab on Morningstar's screen is where you set the criteria for the search. On your first use of the screen, you may encounter some terms you don't understand, although they are all explained in the "light bulb" windows. Don't worry about the terms you don't understand. I'll cover these and more in Chapters 6 and 7.

The best way to use a screen is to start with just a few criteria selected to begin building a list for further refinement. The screen will work with just a few of the variables selected, although you will get a large list. After you've made your first selection, you can view the results and then go back and add in additional variables. Your initial selections are saved until you start a new screen.

For example, if I select Large Core, a minimum market capitalization of $10 billion, and a profitability grade of "A," the Morningstar screen currently returns 55 results. That's a great start, but it's still too many to research in-depth.

The screen allows me to go back to the criteria page and add or change my selections. If I go to the Financial Health choice and click A and B, the screen will look for the same stocks as before but with a Financial Health grade of A or B. Now I am down to 34 stocks. If I ask for a Five-Year Forecasted Earnings Growth of greater than or equal to 10 percent, the screen narrows the field down to 14 stocks. If I add three-year revenue growth greater than or equal to 10%, my screen narrows the field down to two stocks.

Bear in mind this is just an example of how screens work. You must decide what fits your personal financial goals. Also, this same search may yield different results by the time you read this book.

The best way to learn how to use stock screens is to play around with the criteria and observe the results. There are thousands of stocks listed from various public exchanges, and screens are the most efficient way to narrow your search.

When you narrow your search, clicking on an individual company in the results takes you to comprehensive information about the company. When you use the free service, what you see is basically any relevant public information gleaned from company filings. You'll also see links to other information, usually identified by a "+" sign. This indicates the information is for premium members only.

As you become more familiar with the terms used in the stock screen, you will be able to select more criteria on the first search and narrow your results faster. It's important to have a working knowledge of the various numbers and ratios to fully use and understand the screen—all of which are covered in this book.

Summary

Accurate, unbiased information to inform your stock investing is abundant. Unfortunately, it's swimming in a sea of misinformation, scams, schemes, and get-rich-quick quacks. If you stick with reliable sources, the information you need is there. Avoid hints, tips, and so on from any social media platform, and especially stay away from forums, chat rooms, and so on. Stock indexes serve as a benchmark to compare how your stock picks perform relative to the broader market. Stock screens make finding stocks easier by sorting through thousands of possibilities to find the ones worth investigating more thoroughly. Master this tool, and you're on the way to dramatically reducing research time.

Chapter 4

Financial Statements

If the thought of analyzing financial statements intimidates you, welcome to the crowd. People spend years in college learning to analyze financial statements, and this book will not replicate those years of study. However, you will come away with a better understanding of what the numbers mean and which ones are really important to your analysis.

Financial statements contain the history of what happened to the company during a certain period. The law requires that publicly traded companies provide audited financial statements for review. Accounting firms verify that the numbers are correct and sign the audit.

Although it is certainly possible to play fast and loose with the numbers, investors can be confident that, for the most part, what they are seeing is an accurate description of the company's finances. It's important to note that all financial statements are historical in nature, which means they reflect what has happened in the recent past but say nothing about what may happen in the future.

In upcoming chapters, I will cover several ways to place a value on a company—that is, a fair price for its stock. These valuation processes use numbers from the financial statements to generate their conclusions. It is important that investors have an idea about where the numbers come from, why they are significant, and where there are flaws in the reporting.

Company Reports (Financially) Tell All

Publicly traded companies must provide detailed reports to investors and the Securities Exchange Commission (SEC). These documents contain the three financial statements I discuss in this chapter. The most familiar of these documents is the annual report, which companies are required to file at the end of their fiscal year. Most companies have a fiscal year that coincides with the calendar year; however, some start their fiscal year in months other than January. Apple, Inc., for example, has a fiscal year that ends in September.

The *fiscal year* is a way to define the period covered by a company's financial statements. Most companies use a fiscal year that begins January 1 and ends December 31. Others choose different dates for their fiscal year. For example, Apple's 2022 fiscal year began September 26, 2021 and ends October 1, 2022. Like many other things, Apple does time differently.

The annual report is usually printed in a magazine format with photographs of happy customers and grateful employees. The real meat of the report is not found until near the end, when the three financial statements are presented along with the accountant's certification of accuracy. Some companies will mail you an annual report, and you can often find the details on the company's website under investor relations.

The 10-K is another version of the annual report, but the company is required to file it with the SEC. The 10-K is all business, with none of the glossy pictures and glowing text that are often found in annual reports. The 10-K contains more information and goes into greater detail than an annual report, including reports about risks the company faces. These 10-K repors are freely available at the SEC website. Also, you can download 10-K reports from the investor relations section of the company's website.

The 10-Q is also required by the SEC but is filed quarterly. These can be very helpful because they provide more current information than the annual report or the 10-K. The 10-Q is also available for download from the SEC and some companies' websites. Unlike 10-K reports, most 10-Q reports are unaudited.

Three Main Financial Statements

There are three main financial statements that you will use when analyzing a company. From the statements, you can draw conclusions about the relative health of the company and make some guesses about its financial future. You will find the financial statements in the documents previously discussed.

Following are the three financial statements I cover:

- Balance sheet
- Income statement
- Statement of cash flows

Together these three reports give you enough information to begin a valuation of the business. The three financial statements give you three different views of the company's performance, but they all tie together to make a complete picture.

Accounting Definitions

Accounting is a language unto itself. Accountants define some key terms differently than how the terms are commonly used. I can't provide a complete dictionary of accounting terms, but three stand out. The terms are ubiquitous in the following three financial statements. They are:

- **Income**. When reviewing financial statements, be aware that the term "income" doesn't mean "money coming into the company." Income loosely means "profit" in accounting speak, although there are several types of income. Normal people think of income as what they earn—paychecks, interest on bank accounts, and so on—not the bank balance after you've paid all the bills.

- **Revenue**. Revenue is roughly a synonym for "sales" or, in some cases, "fees collected from customers."

- **Expenses**. A company's expenses include what you might expect: the cost of inventory, labor costs, and so on. However, there are other charges, such as depreciation, that most of us don't deal with in our personal finances.

If you stumble across an accounting term that doesn't make sense, consult an accounting dictionary. Google "accounting dictionary" or go to Investopedia.

The Balance Sheet Must Balance

The balance sheet, also known as the statement of financial position, is a snapshot of the company's financial strength at the end of the fiscal year (10-K) or quarter (10-Q). The balance sheet details what the company owns and what it owes. It does not show money flowing in or out. (That information is on the statement of cash flows.) Instead, a balance sheet gives you a snapshot of whether the business is viable.

It is called a balance sheet because it must balance. The balance is often expressed as this formula:

assets = liabilities + (shareholder) equity

or

(shareholder) equity = assets – liabilities

The three terms that make up the formula—assets, liabilities, and equity—are the heart of what the balance sheet tells you about the company.

Assets: What the Company Owns

Assets represent what the company owns. The expectation is that assets can provide economic value to the company. This can be as straightforward as buildings, real estate, and equipment and materials used for production. Obviously, cash and investments represent assets the company can use.

However, there are other categories of assets that are not so tangible. For example, if a company buys another company, it usually pays more than the actual cash value. The difference is called "goodwill" and represents the value of the acquired company beyond its cash value. For example, if you wanted to buy Apple, Inc., you would pay much more than what the buildings, equipment, and so on are worth. The Apple name and brand would be worth many times the tangible assets it owns.

Assets are also broken down by whether the company plans to use them in one year—called "current assets." Current assets include cash, inventory (in most cases), short-term investments, and accounts receivable. Accounts receivable represent money the company expects to collect from customers but has not received. Accounts receivable is a particularly important number. Companies use accrual accounting to book a sale, even if the customer hasn't paid the bill, as long as there is a reasonable expectation of payment. This number shows up on the income statement as revenue, even though no money has changed hands. It is counted on the balance sheet as an asset because the customer is expected to pay soon. This is an important point to remember when looking at the balance sheet and income statement; however, it does not apply to the statement of cash flows.

Noncurrent assets include property, buildings, and equipment, which represent an economic value but are not expected to be converted to cash. Other assets, another noncurrent asset, may include items such as intellectual properties or other items that may be peculiar to that industry. For example, a bank's balance sheet would feature some different items than those found on a manufacturing company's balance sheet.

Unfortunately, there is no standard nomenclature for balance sheets, so you may see different categories represented on some statements. However, the idea is to capture everything the company owns that is of economic value. The total of all these items is the company's total assets.

Liabilities: What the Company Owes

What a company owes are its liabilities. Like assets, liabilities are divided into current and noncurrent. Current liabilities are bills that must be paid within one year. (Obviously, some must be paid sooner.) Liabilities include bills for materials, parts, or other obligations. Most of these fall into the accounts payable category. Accounts payable is an important number because it represents money that must be paid out quickly. Does the company have the resources to meet these obligations? A reading of current assets will give you a good idea.

Companies have other operating expenses, including the daily cost of running the business: payroll, current taxes, utilities, and so on. All these represent drains on cash, which can be a concern if the company has trouble collecting the accounts receivable. Because of the drain on cash, companies often use short-term borrowing to cover the gap. These are current liabilities, and if the company does huge amounts of short-term borrowing, it may mean trouble.

Noncurrent liabilities represent long-term debt, such as paying off bonds it has issued in the past or long-term financing of plants and equipment. Long-term debt is an important number because it represents a continuing drain on the company's cash. Some types of businesses require more debt than others. For example, manufacturers may need to borrow hundreds of millions of dollars to build new plants and buy new equipment. Service-related companies, such as software companies, may not need that level of long-term debt.

Shareholder Equity: Value to Investors

Shareholder or stockholder equity is value in the company that is owned by shareholders. Remember the formula:

(shareholder) equity = assets – liabilities

A home mortgage is a simple example: the equity in your home is the difference between the fair market value (assets) – the balance of your mortgage (liabilities) = your equity. Unfortunately, if you owe more than your house is worth, you have negative equity. A company faces the same reality. If it loses money, the stockholders' equity could be negative or reduced from the previous year.

A company's shareholder equity section on the balance sheet may have several entries, but retained earnings are the most important. This entry represents the beginning capital that financed the company's start and any earnings that are not paid out in dividends. Some companies pay no dividends, so their retained earnings entry will grow from year to year, as long as they are making a profit. However, most companies use retained earnings to pay off long-term debt, buy new equipment, or otherwise reinvest in the company. Paying for these items out of retained earnings means the company does not have to borrow more money.

The Income Statement Is Home to the Bottom Line

While many investors and the media focus on the income statement (this is where you find the magic "bottom line"), it only provides part of the picture for any business. Still, the income statement reports whether the business made or lost money. It is easy for some to confuse the income statement with their checkbook. Did I take in more than I spent, and if so, did I make a "profit" this month?

As you might suspect, it is a little more complicated than that. The ability to record a sale before the company is paid is only one of the complicating factors that haunt the income statement.

The income statement has three major sections:

- Revenue
- Expenses
- Earnings or income

Look at any income statement, and you will quickly notice that it reports more than one type of profit or income.

Revenue Is Sales

Revenue, or as it is sometimes called, "sales," represents the money resulting from the company's business operations. The income statement may add subcategories based on product lines, countries, or other factors. The 10-K usually labels these revenues as consolidated, meaning the company lumped several businesses or business units into one statement.

The next major item on most income statements is an expense called "cost of goods sold (COGS)." COGS represents the direct expenses that are tied to producing goods or services for sales. For example, COGS includes labor costs, cost of raw materials, and cost of inventory bought for resale or used in manufacturing. Sales expenses, distribution costs, and other expenses not directly related to producing the product or service are excluded from COGS. When you subtract COGS from the sales number, you get gross profit. Although it is not on the income statement, you can calculate an important metric called gross margin. Gross margin is the gross profit as a percentage of revenues. The gross margin lets you compare one company to another in the same business. If a company has a higher gross margin than its competitors, then it is more efficient at making its goods; also, this company may have an advantage in the market because it could lower its price(s) and perhaps capture a larger share of its market from its competitors.

Expenses: The Cost of Doing Business

Next on the income statement are the expenses associated with operating the business. These include selling expenses, administrative expenses, marketing, and research and development. Depending on the business, some items such as research and development or advertising (marketing) may be reported on a separate line. Other expenses are often listed separately. You can find more information on all items in the income statement in the company's 10-K. If the company made money on some nonbusiness-related transaction, it is recorded here and noted in parentheses because this is an expense area.

Also lumped in operating expenses are items such as depreciation, one time charges, and gains. If the company closes a plant, the costs associated with that do not represent ongoing expenses but must be recorded as a charge against earnings. Likewise, the profit from a sale of a product line is a one time event and is recorded as a negative expense. When you deduct operating expenses from the gross profit, you come up with operating income.

Operating Income: Sales Minus Cost of Sales

In its pure form, operating income should be the company's revenue minus the cost of goods sold and operating expenses. This number tells you how much the company made on its business operations and is an important number when analyzing the company. However, as I noted previously, companies can stuff nonrecurring and other one time expenses into the operating expenses, so you need to deduct those from the operating expenses totals to get a true operating income number. Many financial websites make this calculation for you.

Net Income: The Bottom Line

The net income is what most consider the bottom line; however, before you get to that number, there are deductions for taxes, interest expenses, and (income) and other one time expenses or investment income. Yet, this is the number most reported by the company and the media. The net income figure is divided by outstanding shares to arrive at the number of earnings per share (EPS). In Chapter 6, I show you how this metric is used and widely misused.

When you analyze a company, the operating income is more important than the net income because it shows how healthy the business is, especially compared to its peers.

Statement of Cash Flows Tracks Cash In and Out

You seldom hear the media report off the statement of cash flows, but it contains some of the most important information you need to analyze a company for possible investment.

The statement of cash flows details how much cash came into the business and how much went out. The difference is cash left for reinvestment, dividends, and so on. Ultimately, how much cash a company generates after expenses is why you do or don't buy its stock. Companies with a large and growing positive cash flow (more in than out) generate value for the shareholders. A company's future cash flows (projections) help analysts set a value for the stock today because a company is worth the discounted value of future cash flows. I discuss this in more detail in Chapter 6, but for now, it is important to understand where those numbers come from and why they are important.

The statement of cash flows is broken into three parts: cash flows from operations, investing activities, and financing activities. The important thing to remember about the statement of cash flows is that it does not contain nuances, noncash expenses, or other vague accounting actions.

Cash Flows from Operating Activities

This part of the statement starts with net income, which comes right off the income statement. However, remember that net income includes charges for noncash items, such as depreciation, which has to be added back to the statement. Other charges and expenses are adjusted because they affect cash. For example, a pension obligation is deducted from net income because it represents cash leaving the business. Changes in inventory also cause adjustments because a higher inventory level than the previous year takes cash out of the business.

You will notice that the statement of cash flows often lists one or more previous years. This is where changes in inventory, accounts payable, accounts receivables, and so on are reconciled. The change in inventory previously mentioned is seen in the side-by-side listings for the current and previous years. The numbers come from the balance sheet or, in some cases, the income statement. You are looking for how those changes affect the cash flowing through the company. Higher accounts receivable than the previous year means less cash is available, while higher accounts payable (bills the company owes but has not paid) from the previous year means more cash stays in the company. Depending on the type of business, there will be other additions and subtractions from the net income figure. The final adjustment is accounting for any one time, noncash charges that were on the income statement. These could be related to an acquisition or other charges. All of these are found on the income statement and should be added back to the net income.

After all these adjustments, the statement of cash flows produces the net cash from operating activities. This number tells you how much cash the business is generating and is known as "operating cash flow." This is the most important figure on all three financial statements. If a company has a strong and growing operating cash flow, it is probably a serious candidate for investment. Obviously, if the opposite is the case, you may want to walk away without too much more research.

Cash Flows from Financing Activities

If the company pays dividends, they are found in this section. Dividends are how the company returns some of the profits to shareholders. While they represent a charge against cash, dividends are a good thing, and many investors look for companies that pay consistent and growing dividends. The other changes in cash in this section have to do with issuing or repurchasing stock (not every company will have these every year), issuing or repaying long-term debt, and other financing charges. Remember, this statement is about cash in and cash out, so if a company issues bonds, which are long-term debt, the proceeds are added to cash.

What the Statement of Cash Flows Tells You

After all the adjustments (adding in or subtracting out), the statement of cash flows tells you whether the company took more cash in than it paid out for the year. When compared to previous years, it tell you whether cash flows are growing or shrinking. In most cases, you will want to see cash flows growing from year to year, but there may be good reasons for it not to if the company is investing heavily in its growth (new buildings, equipment, and so on). The statement of cash flows pulls together the balance sheet (which is a static, one-day snapshot of the company) and the income statement (which features many noncash expenses and other nonoperating costs and revenue).

Your goal is a company with strong core operations that generates lots of cash after investing in its own growth. The statement of cash flows tells you this information without any of the fuzzy noncash, one time charges found elsewhere.

Summary

Financial statements unlock the mysteries of a company's health and give you a glance at its future. Is the company financially healthy? Is it overburdened with debt or other drags on potential future profits? The answers are found in the balance sheet, income statement, and statement of cash flows. When you have a basic understanding of what these three documents reveal, you have your first look at the potential of an investment (to buy the stock). They can also quickly eliminate potential candidates that fall short of your needs. Understanding what the documents contain will help you make decisions, especially when you use a stock screen, as discussed in Chapter 3.

Chapter 5

Types of Stocks

Stocks can be divided into categories or classes. While you may think in terms of a "technology stock" or a "health care stock," this is just one of many ways to categorize stocks. Another way to organize stocks is by the main reason investors are interested in individual stocks—their attributes in the market. This method is one of the most basic and remains one of the most important methods of organizing stocks.

What is gained by organizing stocks? For one thing, organized stocks can be compared with other stocks in the same category. This is helpful in understanding whether a stock is outside the norm for its category. In this chapter, I look at the most basic categories: growth, value, and core stocks. There are several key metrics that help define the categories, and we'll take a deeper dive into those in the following chapters. I also explain why a company's size (based on its value in the stock market) is an important way to compare stocks. Then I discuss economic sectors and how they play a role in stock selection.

Growth Stocks

Growth stocks are those that take off and never seem to retreat in price—at least that's what investors hope. In truth, no stock rises in a straight line forever—sometimes not even for very long. Even true growth stocks have periods when the price falls back, but the growth pattern resumes eventually, or they cease to be growth stocks, and that's when you move on to another selection. Growth stocks rise faster than the market in general in sales and earnings. Technology stocks, for example, are often labeled "growth stocks."

By their very nature, growth stocks can be exciting and glamorous. The hype surrounding a hot stock can be seductive, but you will almost always be buying at a premium price, which can make it difficult or impossible to turn a profit. The trick is to know the value of the stock and buy or sell based on your determination. There's more about the value (as opposed to the current market price) of the stock. Chapter 6 addresses this distinction.

Growth Stock Characteristics

An important feature of growth stocks is size. In general, a smaller company is more likely to have a growth stock than a larger company. That is not a hard-and-fast rule because some large companies (Amazon, for example) are growth stocks, but it is a good way to begin understanding growth stocks in general. Here are some more important characteristics of growth stocks:

Growth stocks should grow. Growth stocks must grow or fall out of market favor. Growth does not always mean profits. In some companies, market share (growing a customer base) drives investor interest and often the stock's price. Major growth companies may go years without earning a profit but rapidly expand their share of the customer base they serve.

Growth rates usually differ between smaller and larger companies. It's more difficult to maintain rapid growth for larger companies, while young companies may post impressive growth rates, in part, because they start from a relatively low base.

Growth stocks seldom pay dividends. Another important characteristic of a growth stock is that they seldom pay dividends. Growth companies usually require considerable capital to fund expansion and are more likely to reinvest profits (if any) to pay for more growth than pay dividends.

Growth stocks are overpriced. An important characteristic of many growth stocks is that they're frequently overpriced. Growth stocks often command premium prices, which makes it difficult to make money unless you know at what price to buy. Since growth stocks pay no dividends, your profit only comes from selling the stock.

Growth stocks can be volatile. Because investors fall in and out of love frequently with growth companies, their stock prices often bounce up and down, sometimes with breathtaking drama. Growth stocks that disappoint investors by not growing or not growing enough are often dumped quickly, leading to sharp stock price drops.

Growth is not just about stock price. Growth companies post rising numbers in several key indicators. Investors expect rising revenues, rising profits, and a rising stock price. In addition, investors want to see a company post solid returns, such as return on equity and other key measures. However, some young growth companies may go for several years with no earnings (profits) due to the cost of rapid expansion. Many run out of money before ever making a profit.

Growth over peers. Investors want to see the company posting growth rates that match or exceed peers and competitors. By classifying stocks, we can compare them with industry peers and the market in general. A growth company that consistently posts numbers below its peers or competitors would need other compelling reasons to attract many investors.

Growth stocks are generally riskier. The reasons include slowing growth rates, falling out of favor with investors, advances in technology, or other factors that threaten the company's economic market position. Smaller companies are often targets of takeovers by larger competitors anxious to grab market share (takeovers can be good for smaller companies, in some cases, because bidding often boosts stock prices). The brutal reality of the economy and the stock market is that many small companies will fail. However, those that survive have an opportunity to grow into industry leaders.

Taking a Chance on Growth Stocks

Investing in the stock market is about the future, and growth stocks often hold the promise of better than average returns in the future. Unfortunately, that promise of greater returns may be unfulfilled as rising stock market stars slip and fall. One of the most important pieces of making growth stocks work for you is determining when (at what price) to buy and—equally important—when to sell. We'll take a deeper dive into this in Chapter 7.

If you want to invest in growth companies, your challenge is to identify companies that have a reasonably good chance of gaining market share and growing without being taken over by a larger competitor or losing a technology or marketing race. However, smaller companies can be risky. Remember, Apple and Microsoft were both once very small companies.

Value Stocks

The second major definition of stocks is called value stock. Value stocks represent the unappreciated and underappreciated stocks on the market. The companies behind good value stocks are financially healthy and may be doing relatively well in their markets, but for some reason, the stock market does not appreciate the stock's potential. When tech stocks are all the rage, growth investors want tech stocks and not metal fabricators or service or retail stocks. Because they are not in a hot industry sector, value stocks often languish until the market re-discovers their potential.

As unglamorous as value stocks may seem, many investors have done very well carefully looking for those companies trading significantly below their true value. Because most value stocks do not attract attention, there is a good chance you can buy them at reasonable prices. It is rumored that Warren Buffett, the most successful investor in the United States, made investing in value stocks the basis of his investment philosophy.

Not Cheap Stocks

Value stocks are not "cheap" stocks, which indicates their prices are low or the stocks are nearly worthless. The feature that identifies a value stock is the price relationship to the company's real value, as determined by the investor. The share price is only a factor as it relates to other stocks. The term investors like to use is "intrinsic value," and I cover it in Chapter 6. In a nutshell, if you determine a company's intrinsic value is $25 per share, and the stock is priced at $18 per share in the market, you may have a value stock.

Value Stock Characteristics

Value investors look for stocks with certain characteristics. There is no universally accepted definition of value stocks, so you may see other characteristics identified than the ones listed here. The point is to develop a profile of a value stock, so you can judge stocks on the same basis. Some of the terms may be new to you, but don't worry; I'll cover them in more detail in Chapter 7. And you shouldn't stress over any math involved in these numbers; they are all readily available on the internet via a good stock screener:

- **Low price/earnings ratio (P/E).** The P/E tells you how the market values the company's share price. A high P/E suggests the market has overvalued the stock price. Therefore you're looking for stocks with a low P/E. Look for stocks in the bottom 10 percent of all similar companies. If a company has no earnings (profits), there will be no P/E.

- **A low earning/growth ratio (PEG).** Most analysts look for stocks with a PEG of less than 1. PEG uses an estimate of the company's growth, which means some analysts will arrive at a different PEG. The PEG is calculated by dividing the P/E by an estimate of the earnings-per-share growth. This metric is readily available on websites such as Morningstar. A low PEG indicates the company is undervalued.

- **There should be at least as much equity as debt.** This information is found on the balance sheet and indicates that debt will not be a significant drag on growth and earnings.

- **High current assets.** Look for companies with current assets that are twice its current liabilities. This is another sign that the company can withstand strains of adverse market conditions, such as a general economic decline or problems in its market segment.

- **A high dividend yield.** The dividend yield is how much the company pays in dividends divided by the share price; the dividend yield is expressed as a percentage. This is a squishy area since there may be good reasons the yield is not high, and some judgment is required. A high dividend yield may mean the company is not reinvesting enough in future growth. The dividend yield is not strong enough to be the single deciding factor in an investment decision.

Don't worry about memorizing all the basic numbers. Just get a general sense of what they mean and how to use them. The actual numbers are available for all companies for free on many financial websites, such as Morningstar.com or Yahoo! Finance. When you have some experience with stocks, you may want to add to or subtract from this list. For example, some value investors want to see the stock hit a 52-week low as part of their screening.

The Value Stock Investor

As with value stocks, the value stock investor exhibits certain characteristics in the way they buy and sell. They place a higher value on the company's fundamentals. A detailed understanding of financial ratios helps you compare a company with its peers. Hard-core value investors stick to a rigid investment strategy. Here are some of the characteristics of a value investor:

Loves the businesses they buy. Value investors tend to be passionate about the companies they invest in, wanting to know all the details about the company, including financials, market strategy, and more. While this passion can help motivate the value investor, be careful that it doesn't blind you to shortcomings or warning signs.

Understands the businesses they buy. The value investor does their homework and can explain what the company does (how it makes money), what its market is, and what companies are competitors. You should know enough to see how the company fits into the economy, where it is strong, and where it is vulnerable.

Looks for great management. Great companies have great managers. Great managers make decisions more like owners than caretakers. Often, strategic decisions that help the company in the long-run impact short-term numbers. Owners do what is best for the company's long-term future.

Frequently reviews their decisions. Value investors often don't own a large number of stocks because analyzing the businesses and frequently reviewing for any changes is time-consuming.

Allows for a margin of error. Finding a good value stock involves a certain amount of unknowns that must be estimated (earnings growth, for example). For this reason, many value investors provide themselves with a margin of error because some of their assumptions may be incorrect. For example, your analysis suggests the stock has an intrinsic value of $25 per share.

Rather than set that as a target price, you provide a margin of error of $3 per share, which makes your target $22 per share. That's the price you buy at. How much of a margin an error you use is determined by how much risk you're willing to endure.

Long-Term Buy

Value stocks are long-term buys that fit nicely into most investors' plans. If you have picked a great company with a stock that is languishing, be willing to hold the stock until other investors discover the same thing. As with all your stock buys, check on the company quarterly to make sure it is still the great company you bought.

Value stocks—even when other investors discover them—tend to rise over time, rather than shoot through the roof. A benefit of owning some value stocks is they often pay dividends. This income may make it easier to hold a stock that is not climbing dramatically in price.

Core Stocks

As you might guess from the name, core stocks are the foundation for your investment plan. It would be easy to assume that core stocks fall somewhere between growth and value stocks, but that isn't quite right. While they do grow at a fairly reliable rate, they are seldom growth superstars. Because they are popular foundation buys, not only for individuals but also institutional investors, mutual funds, and other big investors, they tend to be fairly priced over time. You will seldom find a core stock dramatically underpriced the way value stocks are.

Core stocks are always large companies and could rightly be called "blue chip" stocks. Think of the 30 stocks that make up the Dow. However, there are plenty of stocks that fit the qualifications for core stocks beyond those in the Dow. Conservative investors may have all or much of their portfolio in core stocks, which is not a bad strategy.

Core Stock Characteristics

Mutual funds and other institutional investors have guidelines for buying core stocks, and you should, too. To help you form your own guidelines for investing in core stocks, here are some of the key characteristics:

Core stocks represent big companies. Large companies tend to be older with mature markets. Size is usually an advantage in competitive markets. While they may not be as nimble as smaller competitors, core companies have financial, marketing, and other assets that help them weather difficult economies and market changes. However, a core stock today may not be a core stock tomorrow. Market trends, changes in technology, and bad management decisions can change the designation.

Core stocks make money. Core stock investors look for companies that are profitable year after year. In addition to regular profits (earnings), great core companies are good investments when bought at the right price. It is this consistent return and the stability of it that earn core stocks their high regard in the investment community. Like any investment strategy, develop a profile of core stocks that fit your goals and frequently monitor them to confirm they still fit.

Core stocks grow. Despite their size, core stocks manage to consistently post growth in revenue and earnings. Core stocks will seldom jump dramatically as smaller companies often do. However, they can be counted on to grow earnings, which usually lead to higher stock prices. Core stocks often pay dividends, which add to investors' returns with annual income.

Core stocks have strong financials. Core stocks tend to have very strong financial statements that reflect relatively little debt, strong cash flow, and other key metrics covered in Chapter 4. They are not going out of business anytime soon. If you've done your homework, the value or growth stock you bought in the past may mature into a core stock.

Safety and Stability

Not all large companies qualify as core stocks because of toxic financial statements, out-of-date products and services, and many other reasons. Look at all of the previously listed characteristics and add some of your own when you become more familiar with investing in stocks.

True core stocks provide a measure of safety and stability to your portfolio. That doesn't mean they are completely safe investments that you don't need to monitor. The stock market graveyard is littered with large companies that failed to protect their market share or lost track of their customers' needs.

The Cost of Safety

Core stocks are attractive to many investors, from individuals to institutional investors, which means you will not find them on sale frequently. When the stock market is declining or the economy is shaky, there is often a "flight to safety," which includes core stocks (also bonds and cash). The movement of capital to core stocks from other investments tends to push up the price. Even when the stock market is excited about a sector or group of stocks, core stocks hold up well in price because conservative investors will not sell just to chase the latest fad.

Size Matters in Stocks

One of the ways you analyze stocks is to compare key metrics to other stocks of the same size and industry sector. I discuss industrial sectors in the next section of this chapter. Company size is important for two reasons:

- **Companies of different sizes behave differently.** A company with sales in the tens of billions of dollars and with thousands of employees will not respond to market conditions the same way as a company with 100 employees and a couple of million dollars in sales. If you want to know if the large company is performing well, compare it to companies of roughly the same size.

- **Large companies are less risky.** Small companies have a high mortality rate, which makes them riskier than large companies. The more risk you take, the larger the potential reward must be. Larger companies are less risky and do not often command a risk premium.

A large company is no guarantee of safety for investors, nor is a small company doomed to failure. However, if you want to minimize risk, stick with larger companies. There are several ways to define the size of a business, such as annual revenue, number of employees, and so on.

Sales or revenue is not a good way to classify stocks. Some companies can generate tremendous sales but fail to make a profit, while other companies may have modest sales but post big profits. Which do you want to own?

The standard way of defining size is market cap. Market cap, shorthand for market capitalization, is a way of defining the size of companies. It is simply the number of outstanding (available shares held by the public) shares of common stock times the stock's per-share price. For example, a company with one million shares of outstanding stock and a per-share price of $10 would have a market cap of $10 million.

Here is how I and many other financial professionals define the market cap ranges:

- Mega-cap stocks—market cap in excess of $200 billion
- Large-cap stocks—market cap from $10 billion to $200 billion
- Mid-cap stocks—market cap from $2 billion to $10 billion
- Small-cap stocks—market cap from $300 million to $2 billion

As you can see, there are some wide ranges in the rankings. For example, large-cap stocks range from $10 billion to $200 billion, and mega-cap stocks start at $200 billion and go up. In 2022, Apple's market cap exceeded $2.6 trillion. Those ranges cover a wide range of sizes. Here's where stock screens can come in handy. Depending on the screen, you can usually narrow the ranges so you are getting a closer comparison than the general market cap rankings provide. This gives you a better idea of how the company compares to others that are close to its size.

Stock Sectors

One of the ways investors classify stocks is by type of business. The idea is to put companies in similar industries together for comparison purposes. These groupings are called "sectors," and you will often read or hear about how certain stock sectors are performing ("Tech stocks up today," for example).

One of the most common classifications breaks the market into 11 different sectors; however, you may see other sector lists that have more than 11. It's not particularly important which list you choose, but stick to one to keep comparisons valid. I like the 11-sector list for its simplicity.

Investors consider two sectors to be "defensive or noncyclical" and the remaining nine to be "cyclical." Let's look at these two categories and see what they mean for the individual investor.

Defensive Sectors Defined

Defensive sectors, also known as noncyclical, include utilities and consumer staples (think energy, food, and toilet paper, for example). These companies usually don't suffer as much in a market downturn because people don't stop using energy or eating. They provide a balance to portfolios and offer protection in a falling market.

However, for all their safety, defensive stocks usually fail to climb with a rising market for the opposite reasons they provide protection in a falling market: people don't use significantly more energy or eat more food.

Defensive stocks do exactly what their name implies, assuming they are well-run companies. They give you a cushion for a soft landing in a falling market. For conservative investors, they offer a relatively stable anchor amid market chaos. Defensive stocks also usually pay dividends and should be considered as a part of your core investments.

Conservative investors favor portfolios with more defensive stocks. This is a fine strategy, but it's not one that will serve young investors, who should be more focused on growing their portfolio. I have more details on building a portfolio appropriate for your circumstances in Chapter 8.

Cyclical Sectors Defined

Cyclical stocks, on the other hand, cover everything else and tend to react to a variety of market conditions that can send them up or down. However, when one sector is going up, another may be going down.

Here is a list of the nine sectors considered cyclical:

Basic materials. Basic materials include those items used in making other goods—lumber, for instance. When the housing market is active, the stock of lumber companies tends to rise.

Capital goods. The capital goods sector contains manufacturers of industrial equipment, defense (as in military) goods, aerospace, construction, and so on. This sector is also very sensitive to the economy.

Communications. These companies are in the telecommunications business as well as wireless (cell phones, for example) carriers.

Consumer cyclical. This sector is very sensitive to the economy. It includes automotive, entertainment, retail, and housing. When the economy is good, these sectors flourish. Not so much in a slow economy.

Energy. This sector includes those companies involved in the exploration for and distribution of natural resources such as coal, oil, gas, and so on, but not utilities.

Financial. The companies in this sector include banks and other deposit-taking companies and stock market participants (brokers, investment banks, and so on).

Health care. The health care sector includes hospitals, clinics, health care management companies, and medical products. Some put this sector in the defensive category because people still need care. However, in tough economic times, people may put off preventive care, for example.

Technology. This sector contains companies that make money on their technology or supplying technology companies. Computer manufacturers, software, hardware, and so on are some of the products they produce. New or significant advances in technology can cause a stir and push this sector up or down.

Transportation. Airlines, trucking companies, railroads, and other companies that move goods or people make up this sector. Energy prices and availability can rock this sector.

Companies in the various sectors may or may not react the same as the whole sector, which can indicate good or poor management depending on the way the company moves.

Summary

There are several ways to categorize stocks that can help you sort and compare like businesses. Growth, value, and core stocks fit different investing goals. Many investors have a mix of the three. Growth stocks offer the chance of big wins but with the corresponding risk of failure. Value stocks are bargains that pay off over time if chosen and bought correctly. Core stocks provide a foundation of solid growth and earnings but few home runs. Investing in large companies is generally safer than buying smaller companies, even with their potential for substantial growth. Understanding the various industry sectors helps you compare similar companies. All of these ways of identifying companies help you with the very important task of asset allocation, which I cover in Chapter 8.

Chapter 6

Stock Price versus Stock Value

How much is a share of stock worth? This is the fundamental question you must answer to successfully invest in stocks. If you don't know what a share is worth, how will you know if you're paying too much or getting a great bargain? The daily price on the stock market is often not much help. Market forces that often have nothing to do with the value of a stock push the daily price up and down. Short-term traders follow prices by the second, in some cases, looking for a quick buck. Long-term investors are focused on buying great companies that will deliver value for years to come. Finding great companies is only half the problem. The other half is buying the stock at a price that offers plenty of room for growth. The stock's daily price in the stock market is determined by many factors other than just the company's value. Arriving at the company's value means considering both the tangible and intangible assets, how well the company protects itself from competitors, and how fundamentally sound its financial statements are.

No Clear Answers on Stock Prices

Determining a stock's price is more complicated than it may appear. In reality, a stock has several prices all set in different ways by different participants in the stock market. How these prices and participants interact is what makes the stock market an interesting and challenging puzzle to solve. Contrary to some perceptions, there is no smoke-filled room where stock market kingpins sit around a table and set prices. Daily prices on the stock market are, for the most part, totally uncontrolled and likely to do almost anything. The price reported by the stock market is just one of several prices investors must deal with. Long-term investors analyze businesses to find a price that represents their fair market value. This number can be very different from the daily stock price. Which price is correct? They both are, actually. The daily price is correct for short-term traders. That price is only relevant when compared to the fair market price determined by long-term investors.

How do you figure a price that represents what the company is truly worth? There are several processes, and most investors use more than one. It would be nice if you could plug in some numbers to a formula and come up with an answer, but it is not that simple. Putting a value on a business—and thus its stock—is part science and part art. If it were not so, everyone would have the same number; however, a quick look at Morningstar.com or Finance.Yahoo.com will reveal a wide range of opinions on most stocks by various analysts.

How Daily Stock Prices Are Set

Stock prices change every time shares are bought and sold. For heavily traded stocks, the price can change several times a second and many hundreds of times during the trading day. So, what causes the price of stocks to rise and fall during the trading day? The media reports that stock prices were up or down based on a particular news event. Whether it is rising inflation or unrest in the Middle East, media pundits want a quick and simple answer to why the market was up or down on a particular day.

Economic news, global news, and other events *do* affect stock market prices. However, these events are just the catalyst for more basic actions and reactions that are the true drivers of daily stock market prices. The simple but powerful forces of supply and demand set stock prices daily. If there are more buyers in the market for a stock than sellers, the price will go up as buyers raise their offers to entice stockholders to sell. If there are more sellers in the market for a stock than buyers, the price goes down as sellers lower the selling price to attract buyers. The balance between supply and demand is self-correcting and happens very fast. This is why the daily price is "correct" for short-term traders.

Ultimately, the price of the stock is equal to what a willing buyer and a willing seller agree upon. However, in the heat of daily stock trading, this price might (or might not) be close to the fair market value. Your job as an investor is to determine the stock's fair market value and compare that value to its daily price on the stock market. This comparison tells you whether it is a good time to buy (or sell) the stock or not. A smart long-term investor waits until the daily price comes to their determination of the stock's true value and doesn't chase a fast-moving target.

Another price that further muddies the waters comes from "experts" who claim some special insight into a particular stock or the whole market. Investors should beware of advice or a tip about a certain stock doubling (or more) in price very soon and that now is the time to go all in to make a killing. The advice is either ignorance or, more likely, the front end of a scheme to take your money. Anyone who "knows" a stock will double in price is illegally trading with insider information, making a guess, or running a fraud.

Price and Value Are Not the Same

Don't confuse price and value when investing in the stock market. Many influences can push and pull a stock's price in daily trading. However, the value of the business is not changed by fluctuations in the stock's price. The value you determine in your analysis establishes the stock's fair market value, at least as far as you are concerned. This fair market value is also called its intrinsic value, which means it reflects the value of the business to investors.

Intrinsic Value Determines Potential Success

Investors who guess at a stock's fair market value will soon find themselves wondering where all their money went because they will not know if they are paying too much for the stock. Smart investors buy a business, not a stock. They analyze the business using proven formulas and arrive at a price for the stock that reflects the value to investors. That price is the stock's intrinsic value, which considers all of the company's assets, both tangible and intangible. When you know the intrinsic value of a company, you can decide whether the stock is overpriced, underpriced, or priced about where it should be. All investors should avoid overpaying for a stock. If this seems like obvious common sense, you are right, but it is not an approach all follow.

Some investors tell themselves all sorts of stories to justify paying more for a stock than its intrinsic value. However, smart investors are patient and wait for a stock that can be bought at a price that gives them a reasonable chance of making a profit. That patience is one of the distinguishing features of a long-term investor. Buying great companies at a great price is the recipe for success.

The process of determining the intrinsic value of a stock involves two broad steps. There is no particular order to the steps. If you encounter major problems with either step, you may want to skip straight to another investment candidate. The two steps are shown here:

1. Determine a price for the stock that reflects its value to investors.

2. Determine if the company has a sustainable economic advantage or moat.

Of the two, analyzing the company's economic moat is a bit more subjective. However, if the company has no economic moat or one that appears unsustainable, I would suggest you pass on that company unless you're an aggressive growth investor. Young growth companies will not have a strong economic advantage. If you're looking for a growth stock, decide how much risk you're willing to accept for a potential future winning investment.

> **Important note for growth investors.** Growth investors will find that younger and smaller companies may fall short in achieving the markers listed in this chapter. Your task is to gauge whether the company is moving toward hitting the recommended levels and what amount of risk you're willing to take to see if it matures to a potential leader. In their early days, most of today's giants would not have scored well. Likewise, hundreds of hopeful upstarts stalled, and many died unceremoniously.

Analyzing a Company's Economic Moat

The terms "economic moat" and "competitive advantage" mean roughly the same thing. Other synonyms exist, but essentially, an economic moat represents those qualities that make the company a leader (or potential leader) in its field with a market position that is easy to defend.

An economic moat protects a company from being overrun by competitors. It is not a guarantee against competitors capturing market share, but its strength can slow them down. A strong economic moat today does not mean it will last forever. In the early days of computers, IBM had a lock on most of the business.

While it is still a strong company, the industry has evolved and is full of competitors. Great companies adapt to changes in technology and its market.

An economic moat is important in determining the company's intrinsic value because it gives you some idea of the potential long-term success of the company. As a long-term investor, you are looking for companies that can deliver value to stockholders for years to come. A strong economic moat is part of the answer to that question. Determining how a strong economic moat protects a company begins with a look at its financial health. The best way to find this information is to visit one of the websites discussed in Chapter 3, such as Morningstar, and find the following suggested indicators. The next step in analyzing a company's economic moat is evaluating how deep and wide it is.

Strong History of Making Money

It is not enough for a company to be profitable today. You want companies that have been making money for years or have a record of strong progress toward profitability. Has the company been profitable or grown in good economies and bad? Has the company grown market share, revenue, or earnings? Does the company generate a strong free cash stream? These are all signs of a company that is at the top of its market or headed that way. Most importantly, do you see signs that suggest the company will continue to grow and prosper? Morningstar shows you five years of history on its free side and ten years on the subscription side. Ten years would be better, but five years will do.

Financial ratios are tools investors use to measure the health of a company. They are also good ways to compare one company to another, and you can compare a company to its peers and industry sector. Most ratios have some flaws, so you should never rely on a single metric.

Here are some markers of profitability:

Earnings growth. Look for companies that post year-to-year growth in earnings (an occasional hiccup during recessions or downturns is acceptable). Although this is not a perfect metric, it is one you should look at. (Remember, accounting adjustments can distort earnings.) Make sure the target company is reporting earnings substantially higher than its major competitors and sector (you can find these numbers in Yahoo! Finance in the stock research section).

Free cash flow. Great companies generate a lot of cash and, particularly, have a large flow of free cash. Free cash is what remains of earnings after the company reinvests in itself to keep the business operating. Another way to think of this is how much cash you could pull out of the business without forcing a change in operations (closing plants, layoffs, and so on). Remember, growth companies may reinvest all or most of their free cash to push growth.

Return on assets (ROA). How efficient is the company in generating earnings? Great companies have a superior return on assets to their sector. This measure tells investors the company is using assets wisely and creating value for the owners. For example, two companies each have $100 in assets. One company uses those assets to create $5 in earnings, while the other company uses the same amount of assets to create $15 in earnings. Which would you choose to own? Compare companies in the same industry and sector for a valid check.

Return on equity (ROE). Another way to look at a company's profit-generating efficiency figures is how the company uses debt in addition to assets. Because most companies use some debt to run the business, it is important to take it into consideration. ROE considers how well the company uses investors' capital and includes debt. It is very important to compare companies in the same sector. If a company has a higher ROE than its sector, be careful that something unusual isn't boosting the number (recent acquisitions, buying back stock, and so on).

Net margin. A company's net margin is simply net income divided by sales. This tells you how efficient the company is in wringing profits out of sales. For example, some industries (grocery stores) have low net margins and must drive a lot of revenue to generate profits. Other industrial sectors have higher net margins thanks to the nature of the business (software, for example). Great companies beat sector averages and close competitors.

If you want to calculate key financial ratios or markers yourself, feel free to grab the latest statements and a calculator. However, you can find all of the key financial facts about a company online, often including historical numbers for reference.

Evaluating an Economic Moat's Width and Depth

All economic moats are not created equal. Some look wide but may be shallow, while others are narrow but deep. Great companies have economic moats that are wide and deep, which provide the best protection and are an indication that a company has a long-term future. There are several key characteristics to look at in evaluating a moat. Admittedly, this is somewhat subjective. You can find comments on these topics on most of the websites I mentioned in Chapter 3 (some may use the term "economic advantage" instead of "economic moat").

Following are key characteristics you should look at when evaluating a moat:

Strong products. Few companies produce anything that is unique in the market, at least not for long if there is money to be made by the product. As soon as patents expire, generic drug makers duplicate leading products at deeply reduced prices. When Apple introduced the iPhone in 2007 and the iPad a few years later, it created a whole new industry. There were other similar products on the market, but these two raised the bar so high that competitors could only produce wannabes for a number of years. Eventually, competitors matched Apple's products, but in the meantime, Apple is making money faster than it can count it. Apple has superior products and a hugely loyal customer base that is difficult to challenge. Great companies have products that competitors can't easily match and customers who keep coming back. Either one (or both) is a wide and deep moat.

Locks out competitors. A strong economic moat can lock out competitors by cutting prices to the bone, while still providing a profit to the company. A classic example of this is Wal-Mart, which has such efficient operations and massive buying power it can, and does, prove fatal to less-efficient competitors. Another way to lock out competitors is to create a high cost to enter the market and be competitive. It takes a tremendous amount of money to start an airline and compete with existing carriers.

Locks in customers. An economic moat can protect a company's customer base by making it difficult or expensive for competitors to entice them away. One way to do this is to make it difficult and/or expensive to switch. Cell phone service providers used this tactic by requiring most customers to sign a two-year agreement with a stiff penalty if they want out before two years. Banks and other financial companies want as much of your financial business (banking, loans, investing, insurance, and so on) as possible, so moving your business would be difficult and inconvenient. Social media companies, such as Facebook, use networking to build a solid moat. You join because your friends and family joined, and then a friend of yours joins and so on. In early 2012, Facebook had 750 million users. Ten years later, that number was 2.9 billion. Yes, a new social networking company may pop up (they do all the time), but it is hard to imagine one duplicating Facebook's success.

Durability of an Economic Moat

How long will an economic moat retain its protection? This is almost impossible to know for sure, but by looking at the industry where the company competes, you may be able to make a guess. We are unlikely to give up toilet paper, food, or energy anytime soon. However, moats built on cutting-edge technology may not be sustainable. Unless companies keep innovating, technology alone is not strong protection—someone is always looking for and finding a better solution. Microsoft became an economic giant on the back of its operating system, which is widely considered far from the best but is installed on some 75 percent of personal computers. Microsoft built on this positioning by introducing a suite of office technology tools (I'm using one right now) that only (at that time) ran on its operating system and are ubiquitous in businesses around the world. Other companies with durable brand names such as Coke, General Mills, and Nike have years of consumer confidence filling their moats.

No moat exists forever or is beyond breaching. All companies, even those with the strongest brand, customer base, and financial strength, must work to maintain their economic advantage. If competitors find a crack in the protection, they will exploit it.

The Next Step: Analyzing the Business

Analyzing a company may seem like a daunting task, and it can be. The key is to focus on the important concerns such as revenues, earnings, and cash flows. Then you will see a clear picture of the company's financial health.

If you are satisfied that the company has a large and sustainable economic advantage, it's time to move on to analyzing the business and coming up with a fair market value (intrinsic value). Two things to keep in mind: the intrinsic value is what the stock price should be if it reflected the true value of the company, and it is also a moving target that will change as the company's financial fortunes change. Finding that number (stock price) will tell you whether the stock is a bargain, priced about right, or overpriced.

Value investors are looking for stocks that the market is pricing significantly below the intrinsic value. Growth investors may be happy with a stock price that is close to the intrinsic value, but the company still has much room for growth. If you are looking for a core stock that you hope will provide a higher stock price in the future and/or a steady stream of dividend income, the intrinsic value tells you if the stock is fairly priced.

Before I dive into valuation, let's look at some of the more popular stock ratios.

Using Ratios in Analysis

You will hear and read a lot about ratios, or multiples, as they are sometimes called. A quick glance at a stock on Morningstar will reveal many different ratios: price/earnings ratio, price to sales ratio, price to book ratio, and so on. While some ratios provide a hint about the company's intrinsic value, most of them are based on the stock's current price. That price can be overstated in the case of a hot growth stock or understated for stocks in languishing sectors. While they have some value to long-term investors, they reflect the market's view of the stock today or for the short term. They tell us little or nothing about the future value of the company.

Earnings per Share (EPS)

Earningse per share is a popular metric and the basis for other ratios. You take the company's net earnings and divide that number by the outstanding shares (EPS = net earnings/ outstanding shares).

The EPS helps compare one company to another, assuming they are in the same industry, but it doesn't tell you whether it's a good stock to buy or what the market thinks of it. For that information, you need to look at other ratios.

Before I move on, you should note that there are three types of
EPS numbers:

- Trailing EPS—last year's numbers and the only actual
  EPS
- Current EPS—this year's numbers, which are still
  projections
- Forward EPS—future numbers, which are obviously
  projections

Price/Earnings Ratio (P/E)

The price/earnings ratio is the most popular of all stock ratios,
at least with the media. You calculate the P/E by dividing the
stock's price by its earnings per share (P/E = stock price per
share/EPS).

For example, a company with a share price of $40 and an EPS of
2 would have a P/E of 20 ($40/2 = 20). This means that investors
are willing to pay $20 in the stock's price for every dollar of
earnings, which indicates this stock may be overpriced if others
in its sector are trading at a lower P/E.

The P/E gives you an idea of what the market is willing to pay
for the company's earnings. The higher the P/E, the more
the market is willing to pay for the company's earnings. Some
investors read a high P/E as an overpriced stock, and that may be
the case. However, it can also indicate that the market has high
hopes for this stock's future and has bid up the price. It almost
certainly means this is not the time to buy the stock.

Conversely, a low P/E may indicate a "vote of no confidence"
by the market, or it could mean this is a sleeper that the market
has overlooked.

What is the "right" P/E? There is no correct answer to this
question because part of the answer depends on your willingness

to pay for earnings. Some investors may consider a company with a high P/E overpriced, and they may be correct. A high P/E may be a signal that traders have pushed a stock's price beyond the point where any reasonable near-term growth is probable.

However, a high P/E may also be a strong vote of confidence that the company still has strong growth prospects in the future, which could mean an even higher stock price. Most long-term investors shy away from stocks that post high P/Es because it may indicate there is little room left for growth in price without much higher risk. The market may also become nervous and abandon the stock, causing the price to fall dramatically. Of course, this may be just the stock a growth investor is willing to take a chance on if other information indicates the stock has the potential to keep growing.

Compare a stock's P/E to its sector and competitors to get an idea of how similar companies are being priced. However, the P/E changes every day the stock closes at a new price and quarterly when new earnings are reported.

Other ratios such as price to book, price to sales, dividend yield, and others are often used to value stocks. While these can tell you whether the stock is trading above its sector or the whole market, they tell you nothing helpful about the value of the business. Ratios are helpful when buying or selling for the short term because the price is more important than the value. However, for the long-term investor, value is more important.

Too many investors become hung up on analyzing all the dozens of ratios generated from the company's financial statements. Bogging down in details is a way to lose focus when identifying great companies and buying their stocks at a great prices.

Intrinsic Value Using Discounted Cash Flows

While ratios offer some information about what the market considers a fair price today, those numbers can be distorted by many factors. The most common method of arriving at the intrinsic value of a stock is using the discounted cash flows method. Discounted valuation models are used to price a number of different assets. The model that most stock analysts use is the discounted cash flows method. It is a complicated process involving some math and assumptions about things such as future revenue, free cash flow, and more. Don't become discouraged by the math and projections. Discounted cash flows is a tool you can use, since many of the resources I mention offer detailed help.

Before I dig deeper into the discounted cash flows model, it is important that you understand the reasoning behind using this process and why it is the favored method of most stock investors.

Understanding Discounting and Future Value

Money has a time value that must be considered with any investment, whether it is stocks, real estate, or something else. Simply stated, the time value of money is that a dollar today is worth more than a promised dollar in a year because a dollar in hand today can be invested for a profit. Equally important, you have the dollar, and there is no risk that you won't have it tomorrow, as compared with the risk of a dollar promised in the future. Many things can happen in a year, which could mean you would not receive the promised dollar or suffer other bad circumstances.

If a dollar today is worth more than a dollar in one year, why would I choose a possible future benefit over a real (dollar) benefit I have in my hand? One way to address this problem is to acknowledge the time value of money. To entice me to wait a year, I must be rewarded. At the very least, in one year, I should receive the equivalent of one dollar today, plus a premium for risking the wait.

The discounted cash flows method for valuing stocks rests on this principle (though from a different perspective). The simple description of discounted cash flows is that a stock is worth the sum of future discounted cash flows. If you project that a company is going to have future free cash flows of 5 percent more than the previous year, you can calculate what each of those cash flows will be (starting with $100) at the end of the following periods:

Year one = $105

Year two = $110.25

Year three = $115.76

Year four = $121.55

Year five = $127.63

However, thanks to the time value of money, you know that each year's cash flows must be discounted, and the farther out the cash flows, the greater the discount.

The discounted cash flows model uses other projections and estimates to arrive at a fair market value for the stock. This is the method preferred by most stock analysts. If you are clever in math and confident that you can predict future cash flows, revenues, and other variables, there are many places on the internet that will show you how to make these calculations.

Following is a basic model from Investopedia.com that is used by many analysts. (There are numerous variations of this formula.)

$$PV = CF1 / (1+k) + CF2 / (1+k)2 + \ldots [TCF / (k–g)] / (1+k)n–1$$

This model is broken down as follows:

PV = present value

CFi = cash flow in year i

k = discount rate

TCF = terminal year cash flow

g = growth rate assumption in perpetuity beyond the terminal year

n = the number of periods in the valuation model, including the terminal year

The Weakness of the Discounted Cash Flows Model

The weakness of the discounted cash flows model is you (and me). The model only works if you have realistic estimates to include on future cash flows, estimated future revenues, discount rates, how much risk is involved, industry analysis, and so on.

There are discounted cash flows calculators on the internet that simply require you to enter some estimates and the program will calculate the number for you. The outcome is only as good as the data you enter. Whether you do the calculations manually or use one of the online calculators, the outcome will still be tainted by the estimates you enter. It is possible to find estimates for many of the variables on the internet; however, it is not always possible to verify how the authors arrive at these conclusions. Among industry professionals, there are often wide differences in estimates and risk factors.

The Strengths of the Discounted Cash Flows Model

The model produces actionable numbers if the inputs are from professional analysts who study the market and study the stock you are researching. The intrinsic value is still subjective because of the estimates, and other professional analysts may see the company differently. However, your best bet for finding a reliable estimate of a stock's intrinsic value is from an expert. It has been my experience that Morningstar provides the best and most consistent information on a stock's intrinsic value.

Researching stocks and companies is easy on the internet, but be very careful of the sources you use. Stick with names and sources you know and trust. The websites listed in Chapter 3 are trustworthy, I believe, and I have no financial interest in them. If a commentator is touting a stock, they should disclose any financial interest in the stock or whether they stand to gain if the price rises.

To access this expertise from Morningstar, you must pay their subscription fee for premium membership. The cost is surprisingly affordable considering the amount and quality of information they provide. Morningstar offers a 14-day free trial. (You must subscribe, but can you can opt out during the 14 days at no cost.) For less than a couple of lattes per week, you can have access to some of the best minds in the business. If you don't like the service, you can cancel. There are other subscription services that may be as good or better, but Morningstar is the one I know and recommend. Morningstar also offers detailed descriptions of how discounted cash flows are calculated for those wanting to do their own math.

Alternative to Discounted Cash Flows Method

What do you use if you don't want to or can't use the discounted cash flows method of valuing a stock? There are other methods for valuing a stock (not valuing the company). The most popular alternative uses various multiples to compare the price of one stock to a comparable stock. The price/earnings ratio (P/E) is the most popular multiple for these comparisons.

The procedure is not unlike using comparable sales to appraise a house for sale. In that case, the real estate agent finds comparable houses in the area that have sold recently and uses that information to help them arrive at a price for your house. The idea is that comparable assets should sell for similar prices. The same process is used for stocks, with the P/E being the common factor.

For example, if you are considering Stock A, which has a P/E of 12, look for comparable stocks (same industry, same size, and so on). If you find three other comparable stocks with P/Es respectively of 18, 17, and 20, you could conclude that Stock A is underpriced because investors are willing to pay more for the earnings of the other three companies.

You can use the P/E formula to find the price based on comparable stocks. Continuing with Stock A, you could average the three comparable stocks to get a target P/E of, say, 18.5. If Stock A had earnings of $2.50 per share, you could calculate a stock price of $46.25 per share (earnings × P/E = price (2.50 × 18.5 = 46.25 per-share price). This is just an approximation, but it should put Stock A on a comparable basis with the three comparable stocks.

This strategy has several flaws, including that the P/E is not always the most reliable of value gauges. The process depends on the three comparable stocks being priced correctly, and there is no guarantee of that. Its biggest flaw is that the process tells you nothing of the company's future value or the stock. If you use this method, and many investors do, you will need to watch the stock more closely and continually measure it against comparable stocks. However, it does not require you to estimate anything or consider multiple variables, which is why it is so popular.

This method is best used to quickly decide whether the stock is underpriced or overpriced. Although you can arrive at a stock price based on the P/E formula, it is not nearly as accurate as the discounted cash flows method. You can also use other key ratios, and all of these can be found on the websites I mentioned in Chapter 3 and xothers.

Other key ratios you can use in valuation include the following:

- Price/Book—Value market places on book value (share price/book value per share)
- Price/Sales—Value market places on sales (share price/ sales per share)
- Price/Cash Flow—Value market places on cash flow (share price/cash flow per share)
- Dividend Yield—Shareholder yield from dividends (annual dividends per share/price per share)

In the end, you will have to decide which method is for you. There is no rule against using both. Whether you calculate your own discounted cash flows or use a service like Morningstar, make sure you have the best guess available on the variables the formula needs. Either way, make a conscious decision to buy a stock based on the valuation method of your choice and not a "feeling" for the stock.

Summary

Long-term investors are interested in the true value of the business, which might be reflected in the current stock price. The daily price of a stock fluctuates depending on the mood of the market at a particular moment. It says little about the long-term value of the company. Determining a stock's true or intrinsic value tells investors whether the stock is correctly priced, undervalued, or overvalued by the market. More importantly, investors can project the stock's intrinsic value into the future using the discounted cash flows method or other tools. This information, along with an assessment of the company's moat or economic advantage, helps an investor decide if the stock is a good long-term risk for the investor's individual goal of finding a good growth, value, or core investment.

Chapter 7

When to Buy or Sell

For the long-term investor, there are three important stock prices:

- The fair market price, which the investor determines through analysis
- The price the investor decides to pay, which may contain a margin of error
- The selling price, which is based on a personal need or goal

All other price movement by a stock is not relevant and may confuse or frighten an investor into making a hasty decision. Always buy a stock with a plan to sell when predetermined conditions are met. With a plan, you are less likely to be distracted by market news that is only relevant to stock prices for a few days. A plan lets you make a sell (or buy) decision based on logic. You're less likely to panic sell during a downturn or make your initial buy during an upturn. Although it may seem overly simple, you will make money investing in stocks if you buy at the right price and sell at the right price. It's as simple as that. However, nothing is ever simple when your money is involved.

The stock market is notorious for allowing investor emotions to drive stock prices in crazy directions. Long-term investors plan for their stocks to grow and add value year after year. However, things change, and companies either adapt or they cease being great companies. (And once they cease being great companies, you must reconsider your ownership of their stocks.) Because the future is unknown, the best you can do is identify great companies you want to own, find a price that fairly represents the company's value, and hope for an opportunity to buy below or near that price. In the end, investing in stocks for the long term is a matter of planning for the best and preparing for the worst.

Don't Follow the Crowd

Despite all the news about computer trading programs that use sophisticated software to make buy and sell decisions, there are still humans involved in the daily ebb and flow of stock market prices. Humans, many of whom want to be as unemotional as a computer program, are still driven by two basic emotions: fear and greed. When these emotions take over the market, logic is replaced.

These powerful emotions can spread and infect otherwise rational people. There are many examples of what happens when emotions overrun logic. The classic example is the dot-com boom of the late 1990s that drove the stock market to put insanely high prices on companies that were little more than a rough outline written on a napkin. Companies that had no products or services, much less profits, were bid up to unreasonably high prices (greed). In March 2000, the stock market woke up and realized most of its newly found darlings would never produce a usable product or service.

As investors fled the market, indexes such as the Nasdaq fell into what appeared to be a bottomless hole. In a very short time, it lost more than half of its value. The Dow and the S&P 500 also suffered severe drops. During a short period, trillions of dollars' worth of value disappeared from the stock market. The inflated values of the tech stocks burst like the balloon they were and the fear of loss drove a selling frenzy.

Don't Follow the Buyers

When greed overtakes the market, traders no longer care what price they are paying for a stock. They ignore valuation and any other logic in favor of a strategy that says there will always be someone else who is willing to pay you more than you paid for a stock (also known as the "bigger fool" strategy). As the stock market becomes excited about the possibility of rapidly rising prices, amateur investors decide this is a time they want to invest in the stock market (greed). Unfortunately, they lack the tools or strategy of professional short-term traders who welcome them to the market as a new source of profits—also known as dumb money.

This pattern repeats itself time and time again. The lesson for long-term stock investors is to stick with buying great companies at great prices.

Don't Follow the Sellers

Fear is more powerful than greed. This has been demonstrated time and time again with a variety of studies, but it can be summarized with the following point: If I told you an investment had an 80 percent chance to make money, most people would be favorably inclined to buy. However, if I said the investment had a 20 percent chance of losing money, most people would say that is too risky and would decline. Obviously, this is the same investment referenced two different ways. Fear of loss is a tremendous power that often overcomes common sense and causes long-term investors to make dangerous mistakes.

When the market is in a steep decline, for whatever reason, the media notes how many people are cashing out of stocks and stock mutual funds. The deeper the decline, the more people flee to the supposed safety of cash or bonds. When prices are falling, investors forget that owning stocks is a long-term strategy. The stock market always has periods of decline and periods of growth. This is why stocks are not good choices to meet financial goals that have deadlines fewer than five years out.

Professional boxer Mike Tyson reportedly said, "Everyone has a plan until they get punched in the mouth." When the stock market punches you in the mouth, you must have patience and courage to act rationally and stick to your plan.

During the market decline beginning in 2007 and finally bottoming in March 2009, thousands of investors sold their stocks and fled to the sidelines. Smart investors took one of two routes during this period: They rode out the decline, or they bought when prices were low and added to their holdings. Both strategies meant it was very likely they came out of the decline in 2012 in a much better position than the investors who sold as prices fell and bought as prices rose. Historically, investors who ride out the dips do better in the recovery than those who sell during the decline and try to buy back in during the recovery.

The COVID-19 pandemic slammed the economy and the stock market in March 2020. It looked as though everything had collapsed in the panic over the tens of thousands of deaths and an economy that shut down. Panic selling in the markets drove the major indexes to lows. Yet, the market righted itself and went on to record highs. These highs were short-lived as the pandemic continued to disrupt the economy and rising inflation and the invasion of Ukraine by Russia shook markets at home and abroad. Regardless of what foreign and domestic issues do to stock prices, the long-term investor must have confidence that great companies will ultimately be a safer choice than trying to outguess the winds of change that will always create new highs and gut-wrenching falls in market prices.

It's important to note that in any decline and recovery, not all companies recover at the same rate and some may not recover at all. This is why you have a plan and a means of checking the financial health of your investments. The pandemic hurt some industries and helped others. Food and entertainment companies have not yet recovered, while Amazon and other online services took off like rockets.

A Planned Approach to Buying and Selling

Successful stock market investors have a plan for each stock they buy. The process starts with identifying the stock and determining a fair market (intrinsic) price for it. You then analyze the company's economic advantage (economic moat) to determine if it is wide and deep enough to provide protection for the foreseeable future. After satisfying yourself that you have a realistic fair market price that accurately values the company and includes an economic moat, your next step is to decide what the top price is you want to pay.

Margin of Error

No matter how hard you work at determining a fair market price, you need to allow for the possibility that you or a service like Morningstar could be wrong. After all, the price was derived from a formula that relied on estimates of future cash flows and other variables. If you used the comparable method of valuation, your price might be more at risk of being wrong. Either way, smart investors include a cushion called a margin of error in the price they are willing to pay for a stock. Here's how it works:

For example, you have done your due diligence and are convinced the stock has a strong economic moat, and you are comfortable with a fair market price of $30 per share. However, you want some protection against the possibility that $30 a share may not be the right price. You discount the $30 price by a percentage to your new price. How much of a discount is a matter of personal preference, but many investors use 15 to 20 percent. A more conservative investor might choose 20 percent or more, while other investors might choose the lower discount.

Assuming you think the margin of error should be 20 percent, your target price is now $24 per share (30 × .20 = 6). That is the most you will pay for this stock. As you can see, this conservative approach may eliminate many stocks from consideration. The patient (and successful) long-term investor will wait for the stock's price to drop to this level before buying, and if it doesn't drop to the target, the investor doesn't buy. The temptation, especially after a lot of hard work, is to buy the stock even if it is not at or below the target price. Of course, this defeats the purpose of the margin of error, and your buy becomes much riskier.

A smaller margin of error may bring the target price closer to where the stock is currently trading, but you must accept the possibility that you may still pay too much for it. If you pay too much, it may be difficult to realize the level of return you anticipated. Growth and value investors have somewhat different views of this process, which I discuss in the next section.

There are various stock market orders that will help you buy the stock at the price you want. They tell your broker at what price to buy the stock, so you don't have to watch the market constantly to get the price you want. I talk more about orders in Chapter 9.

Creating a Buy Plan

Before you buy a stock, you should be able to state, in writing, the reasons for buying it. This is known in the business as a "buy case." A buy case is a simple, to-the-point summary of why this stock makes sense for your portfolio. It covers important points about the company and the stock and forces you to do your homework before investing.

Your buy case will come in handy if the stock takes a tumble. It provides a reminder of why you bought the stock and a checklist to see if the company still meets your standards. If something has fundamentally changed with the company, you have the tools to move forward. Follow this procedure or one similar to it, and you'll avoid buying (or selling) as an emotional response. Though you can add others, here are some points your buy plan should cover:

- *What does the company do?* If you can't explain the major business activity of the company in two or three sentences, you shouldn't be investing in it.

- *What part of the economy does this business serve, and is it growing?* Does the company own or can it capture a large share of that market? What is its competitive advantage (economic moat)?

- *Is the company riding a demographic or economic trend that has long-term implications?* Companies that serve retirement needs of baby boomers have a 76-million-plus market. Companies that define their market too narrowly might limit their potential growth.

- *What do you see that makes you believe the company has room for sustained growth?* Why do you believe the company is in a good position to grow, and why is the stock not priced to reflect this potential? Maybe the stock has been beaten up because of some bad company news you judge to be temporary. Maybe the sector is out of favor and generally depressed. Whatever the reason, you should have a reasonable answer for why the stock price is lower than it should be.

- *Is the company financially sound?* Does it have solid earnings growth? Low debt for its industry? Strong, free cash flow?

When you have built a convincing buy case (at a certain price), you are ready to invest. Retain the buy case and review it at least once a year or more often if the stock takes a big hit to see if any of your assumptions or conclusions have changed.

When you build a buy case before buying a stock, you force yourself to make a rational decision. Investing on instinct is the same as guessing. Sometimes you'll be right, and sometimes you'll be wrong—not a great path to a solid financial future.

When to Buy Different Types of Stocks

Any stock you buy should follow the same guidelines listed previously and the same pricing procedure detailed in Chapter 6. However, there are some differences in the types of stocks you buy and the timing of the purchases. Every investor needs to own a group of core stocks, which are large, market-leading household name stocks. Some investors satisfy this requirement with an investment in index mutual funds. Exchange-traded funds that track major market indexes will work also. However, this is a book about investing in individual stocks, so I discuss this requirement in that context.

When to Buy Core Stocks

Core stocks are the bedrock of your portfolio. These are the stocks that inspire confidence in their ability to earn a decent return and weather stormy markets better than most of the market. When times are uncertain, investors turn to core stocks for their stability. For example, a major beverage and snack company dropped during the 2008 financial crisis, but it never dropped as far as the whole market and rebounded ahead of the market. Likewise, when the pandemic hit the stock market hard in March 2020, it bounced back higher than the broad market, and it paid a consistent dividend through the whole mess. (This example is based on a real company.)

Core stocks should be among your first buys if you are building a portfolio from scratch and your next buy if you don't own several core stocks already. Chapter 8 details how you can build a portfolio that fits your personal situation. A good portfolio for you is not necessarily right for everyone.

Not every large stock qualifies as a core stock, and even some previous market leaders, while still large, have lost the edge that made them great companies. You still must do your research and not just buy one of the components of the Dow Jones Industrial Average (the Dow) and call it done.

When to Buy Growth Stocks

In general, one of the best times to buy growth stocks is during a market dip. If you have done your homework and believe the company is a solid prospect, buying during a market downturn might be a good idea. Investors generally don't like growth stocks that don't grow or don't grow fast enough. If you are convinced the company's growth is just temporarily stalled, consider buying when others are selling.

Growth stocks can be added as your resources and opportunities allow. Like all of your stock purchases, the buying price is critical. However, growth investors are often lax with their research and assume strong growth will overcome any mistakes in the price paid. Wouldn't you rather see that growth add value to your holdings rather than correct your mistake of overpaying?

When to Buy Value Stocks

Successful value investors (and there are some that buy nothing but value stocks) are rigid in their price requirements. They have a plan and stick to it, even if that means they must pass on ten stocks before finding one that meets their standards. A value investor is convinced (by their research) that the company is solid and underappreciated by the stock market. Patience and persistence define value investors.

Have a Plan to Sell Stocks

Successful investors have a plan to sell each stock they own. This plan covers market circumstances such as a significant drop or rise in the stock's price. It also details when you might want to sell for more personal reasons. Either way, the sell plan is in place, so if circumstances change rapidly, you don't have to make an uninformed decision. This is not a long document; instead, it's a series of short statements something like this:

> "If the stock drops X percent, I will (sell or add to my holdings)."

> "If the stock rises to $X, I will sell Y number of shares or all shares."

You get the idea and know what fits your personal financial situation. Here are some reasons for selling you may want to include in your plan:

Risk tolerance reached. You bought a company that looked like a steady, growing concern, but instead, the stock has turned out to be a rollercoaster ride. For whatever reason, this stock is just too volatile for your nerves. Dump this firecracker and replace it with a stock that will let you sleep at night.

You need cash. An unexpected major bill can sabotage anyone's budget. Using a stock, especially one that is underperforming, to solve a financial emergency is another reason to sell. However, take a close look at your personal finances. An emergency cash fund that is not tied up in investments is recommended to avoid, except in extreme cases, liquidating stocks to pay bills.

Moral, ethical conflicts. More and more investors are becoming concerned about the social, environmental, ethical, and moral standards of the companies they own. You may decide that a company you own has practices or products that conflict with your social, religious, or moral beliefs. There is no better reason to sell if that is important to you.

The grass is greener. There is nothing wrong with dumping an underwhelming stock for a company that offers better returns. Long-term investors should avoid dumping carefully researched stock because the price has slumped. If the company still passes your buy case, look (and think) before you leap. The attractive stock you don't own may be a flash on the market, only to fall hard. It is easy to suffer "buyer's remorse" after making a major stock purchase. Suddenly, you doubt your decision, and some other stock looks more appealing. Remember your buy case and refer to it to ease your anxiety.

You've reached your goal. It worked. Your plan to reach that financial goal, whether it is retirement or getting a child through college, was successful. Now is the time to start systematically liquidating those stocks you've tagged for this goal.

The stock drops by X percent. Your sell plan should address this situation. You have several basic choices. You can sell all the stock you own and move on to another stock. You can sell part of the stock you own to take some money out of it but hold on to some shares in case they rebound. You may also decide to do nothing as long as you still believe in the company.

The company flounders. This is your signal to sell. You bought the company because of its fundamentals and its business plan. When something changes, and the company loses its way, you re-examine whether it is the same company or not. The company may find itself out of step with its industry and loses its leadership position.

When a stock is overvalued. Can there be too much of a good thing? There certainly can in the market. When stocks are pushed way past their true value, they are often set up for a fall. Selling an overvalued stock is certainly preferable to buying an overvalued stock. Just be prepared to watch it keep going up after you sell, as happens sometimes. Don't second-guess yourself; it could have more easily gone the other way.

Rebalancing your portfolio. You have decided that the best asset allocation for your circumstances is 60 percent stocks, 30 percent bonds, and 10 percent cash in your portfolio. Good fortune has smiled on you and your stocks, which are now valued at 75 percent of your portfolio. As tempting as it might be to stay there, your best move is to rebalance your portfolio by selling off some of your stocks and bringing the percentages back into alignment. Chapter 8 covers asset allocation and rebalancing your portfolio.

Taxes and Investing

Holding down investment expenses and reducing gains is a major concern for all investors. Expenses fall into two categories: direct investing expenses (broker commissions, for example) and taxes. I cover investing expenses in Chapter 9. When and how you buy and sell stocks is controlled by the taxes that you pay or avoid when investing. There are two major forms of taxation on investors: capital gains and dividends. However, before I discuss taxes directly, there are strategies to avoid some taxes and defer other taxes until much later.

Choosing to Defer Taxes

Taxes are a part of our lives, and there is no getting around that fact. That said, there is no legal or moral reason for you to pay any more than you are legally required to pay. With some planning and foreknowledge, you can keep your tax bill for your stock investing to a minimum.

This is not about tax dodging or evasion, nor is it a substitute for competent tax counsel. I have an agreement with my tax attorney friends—I don't practice tax law, and they don't sue me. So far, it's working out pretty well.

One strategy is to place as much of your stock investments as possible into a tax-qualified account. Tax-qualified accounts, such as 401(k) plans and the various IRA accounts, allow your investments to grow tax-deferred (or tax-free in the case of Roth accounts). This means that as long as your investments and any income, such as dividends or profits from sales, remain in the tax-qualified account, you pay no taxes on current gains. In regular tax-qualified accounts, you don't pay income or other taxes until you begin withdrawing money, presumably in retirement. This allows more of your money and earnings to remain and benefit from compounding. There are various rules and regulations you must follow (and even more for Roth accounts) regarding withdrawals. In most cases, if you wait until you are at least 59½, you avoid any penalties of withdrawing from a tax-qualified account. I can't cover all the issues with qualified accounts, but it is well worth your efforts to learn more from competent tax advisers.

Tax rates are subject to change, and the tax code is even more so inclined. Don't make any tax decisions without consulting a qualified tax adviser who is current on investment tax regulations.

Taxes and Investing in Stocks

There are two main ways income or profits from investing in stocks may be taxed:

- Capital gains tax
- Dividend income tax

Capital gains tax. A capital gain occurs when you sell an asset for a profit. That asset could be a house, land, machinery, stock, or a bond. When that happens, you have experienced a capital gain. You figure the capital gains tax on the difference between your "basis" in the stock and the sales price. This difference is your profit or loss. Usually, the basis is what you paid for the stock. However, if you inherit the stock, the basis is different.

If the difference between the basis and the sales price is negative—in other words, you lost money—you have a capital loss, which you can use to offset capital gains in some cases.

There are two types of capital gains:

- Long-term capital gains
- Short-term capital gains

It is very important to understand the difference and why one is better than the other:

Long-term capital gains. You must hold the stock for at least one full year to qualify for the long-term capital gains rates. This is extremely important, and I encourage you to make absolutely sure by holding the stock for at least one year and a day. The tax on a long-term capital gain is taxed on a graduated scale based on your income. Please check with a qualified tax adviser to learn more about these ever-changing rules.

Short-term capital gains. If you hold a stock for less than one year before selling it, the IRS classifies the sale as a short-term capital gain and taxes the profit as ordinary income. This means you could pay the highest personal tax rate based on your tax bracket. This might be higher than the long-term rate, so consult that tax adviser I keep talking about.

Unless there is a compelling reason, hold on to the stock long enough to qualify for the long-term capital gains rates.

In some cases, a short-term or long-term capital loss can offset all or part of the tax on another transaction.

Dividend tax. Companies that distribute profits through dividends create a taxable event for you. The IRS taxes dividends as ordinary income. Of course, there are exceptions. Otherwise, dividends may be considered ordinary income and taxed at your current rate. There is not much you can do to avoid some tax on dividends. Please find someone smarter than me to help you untangle the tax code.

Summary

Always have a plan when you buy a stock and when you sell it. Your plan helps you avoid irrational decisions based on a market running amuck. The plan defines what needs to happen before you buy or sell and lets you ignore the crowd-think that is often wrong. Depending on your investment strategy, different circumstances could define the best time to buy core, value, or growth stocks. Nobody enjoys paying taxes, so familiarize yourself with tax law basics concerning selling stocks and collecting dividends.

Chapter 8

Building a Portfolio

You absolutely need a plan for buying and selling stocks; however, those decisions should fit into a broader plan for your entire portfolio. Buying great companies is the way to find great stocks, but how those stocks fit into your total holdings is as important as the stocks you buy. When you take the idea of core, growth, and value stocks and combine them with small, mid, and large sizes, you quickly see that there are many possible combinations. When you consider the industrial sectors every company belongs to, you see that you have even more possible outcomes. A strategy called asset allocation provides a map to construct a plan to include the correct combination of assets to reach your financial goals.

Understanding Asset Allocation

Asset allocation is the thoughtful use of assets (investment capital) to balance risk and reward across your holdings. Typically, investors have three classes of assets: securities (stocks, mutual funds, and so on), fixed-income assets, and cash. This is where you should start. More sophisticated forms of asset allocation add other classes of assets such as real estate, precious metals, and so on. The vast majority of investors need only concern themselves with the three basic classes.

Asset Allocation and Diversification

Diversification is often used as a synonym for asset allocation, but it has a narrower focus. Asset allocation and diversification are both strategies to reduce risk. Asset allocation involves how all three asset classes work together to manage risk and improve returns. Diversification refers to how you structure each class for the best results. For example, asset allocation looks at the percentage of each asset class in your portfolio (stocks—60 percent; bonds—20 percent; cash—20 percent). Diversification considers how you spread your stock investments over several industrial sectors (tech—10 percent; financial—35 percent; retail—15 percent; consumer goods—15 percent; utilities—25 percent).

As I note later in this chapter, the correct asset allocation to meet your goal is a fluid process that changes with your risk tolerance and years remaining to reach your goal. Diversification ensures that your portfolio is not heavily weighted in a single sector or industry that will will cause significant damage if the market turns against it.

The Importance of Asset Allocation

As "jargony" as asset allocation sounds, it is incredibly important to your success as an investor. Many studies confirm that correct asset allocation is as important as the securities you buy, possibly more so. Even if you pick the best stocks and other assets, you still may not achieve the return or level of risk you expected if your asset allocation is wrong.

This is because stocks and bonds (the fixed-income asset class in most cases) frequently, but not always, move in different directions. Economic circumstances that drive down stock prices tend to increase the value of bonds. When stocks are rising, the value of bonds often suffers. If you have a good balance, your portfolio may not suffer as much if one asset class drops because another is likely to rise. The opposite is also true: If stocks take off on a steep rise, you may not achieve the same results with a portfolio balanced with all three asset classes because bonds may fall in value. This is the trade-off that reduces risk but limits the upside. If you always know which asset class is about to move up or down, you don't need this book.

This is the balance between risk and reward that asset allocation brings to your portfolio. Because the future is unknowable, your best chance of success is to build your portfolio with an asset allocation that achieves the balance between risk and reward that is comfortable for you. There is no one "correct" asset allocation. Investors must decide for themselves what makes the most sense for their circumstances and tolerance for risk.

Many of the websites I mentioned in Chapter 3 have tools that will let you view how a portfolio of stocks, bonds, and cash may perform as you change the percentages of each asset class. This is helpful for giving you an idea of whether a particular portfolio is best for you.

Those Other Two Asset Classes: Fixed Income and Cash

Although this is a book about investing in stocks, it is impossible to talk about portfolios and asset allocation without touching on fixed income and cash. Making good decisions about these two asset classes is important to your success. They both play a role in the balance between risk and reward.

Why Include Cash?

Cash is included as an asset class because it is the steadiest and most liquid of all investment vehicles. That may seem obvious, but running short of cash in your investment portfolio may mean scrambling to pay for an opportunity you identify that works for your strategy (not a tip from your neighbor on a hot stock). It also means you have resources for emergencies such as loss of a job or a major health crisis. As you enter retirement, cash can pay for daily expenses or that dream vacation. Cash doesn't pay much in the way of a return. In periods of very low interest rates, cash may not keep up with inflation, so it is actually losing some value. You can park your cash in the following places:

- Bank accounts
- Money market mutual funds
- Very short-term Treasury Bills

Fixed-Income Securities (Bonds)

Fixed-income securities provide a steady income and/or a fixed return at maturity. Bonds often move in the opposite direction of stocks, so when stocks are down, bonds tend to rise and vice versa. Bonds are debt instruments; you are lending money to the bond issuer in exchange for a stated return. Bonds are the preferred fixed-income asset class for asset allocation purposes because they come in a variety of maturities and with varying degrees of risk. Bonds pay a fixed interest rate until maturity, when all of your investment is returned. Bonds are rated for their security by outside companies. More risky bonds pay a higher interest rate to attract borrowers willing to take more risk. Rule of thumb: The longer the maturity (when you get your investment back), the higher the interest rate. With the exception of U.S. Treasury issues, all bonds may default, meaning you lose some or all of your investment. There are basically three issuers of bonds ranked in terms of general safety:

U.S. Treasury issues. Treasuries, as they are known, are the gold standard for virtually risk-free investing because they are backed by the full faith of the U.S. government, which can print money or raise taxes to cover its oblgations. The Treasury issues bills, notes, and bonds with maturities ranging from days to 30 years. For conservative investors, these are the securities of choice. The absolute safety of your principal comes with a price: Treasuries pay the lowest return of all bonds.

Other government entities. Frequently known as a municipal bond or muni, these bonds are issued by governmental entities other than the federal government. State and local government units use the bonds to finance roads, bridges, water infrastructure, and other public needs. They also have a variety of maturities. Income from municipal bonds is low, but not as low as treasuries. They are not as safe as treasuries and some may be risky, depending on the financial health of the issuer.

Corporate bonds. Companies issue bonds to raise money rather than sell more stock and dilute the ownership. The bond market is usually a better place to borrow long term than banks or other lenders. Corporate bonds range from very secure to highly risky, so know what you are doing before you buy a corporate bond.

Buying individual bonds can be tricky for the uninformed—except for treasuries. Many investors use a bond index mutual fund or a bond index exchange-traded fund to meet their bond asset class requirement.

Bonds would require a whole book to explain in detail, but this brief overview will place them in context for our discussion on portfolios.

Timing Is Everything

Building a portfolio begins with an understanding of how much time you have to reach your financial goal—for most of us, a secure retirement. If you were (are) smart, you started saving for retirement as soon as you started your first adult job. Of course, most of us weren't thinking about retirement as young adults. Starting young and staying with a retirement program is the best way to reach that goal. If your employer offers a retirement program such as a 401(k), sign up on day one and contribute what you can, but certainly up to the maximum percentage your employer matches.

For people still 30 or more years away from retirement, it makes sense to be as aggressive (but not crazy) with your portfolio, given your tolerance for risk. If you make a mistake or the market turns against your aggressive stocks, you have time to recover. However, if you have fewer than 15 years before retirement, be much more conservative with your stock investments. At this stage of life, preserving what you have becomes as important as hitting aggressive growth goals. Think of asset allocation like an accelerator on a car. When people are young, they drive fast and take chances. Older drivers slow down and become more cautious—at least they should. This is how your investments should work too.

How to Build a Portfolio That Fits You

Building a portfolio starts with an understanding of the relative risk associated with the possible combinations of asset classes. Using this understanding, you can fit the pieces together to build a portfolio that addresses your financial goals and is within your risk tolerance. You should never buy a stock(s) or put together a portfolio that keeps you awake at night because it is too risky.

Stocks Asset Class

As a broad rule, stocks are riskier than bonds. As with most generalities, it is easy to poke holes in a flat statement. Top-quality companies (core stocks) are less risky than very poorly rated corporate bonds. However, within the continuum that includes all stocks, some are riskier than others. Growth stocks tend to be riskier than core stocks. Value stocks may or may not be riskier than growth stocks.

The size of the company matters a great deal when assessing risk. Small company stocks are riskier than large company stocks. Stocks in certain industrial sectors may be more risky than stocks in other sectors. Tech stocks are often riskier than other industrial sectors because technology can change quickly—today's leader can be tomorrow's also-ran. However, economic circumstances can move almost any industrial sector into the risky column. For example, during the housing collapse that began in 2007, homebuilders took a devastating blow, as did major appliance makers and so on. The COVID-19 pandemic that clobbered the markets in March 2020 caused lingering problems for the entertainment and travel industries, among many others.

When you put company size and industrial sector together, you get pieces of the allocation puzzle that fit into specific slots. For example, small tech companies are generally considered risky, even when the sector is doing well, so they may have a place in an aggressive portfolio. Very large, well-diversified companies (core stocks) work in almost every portfolio to some extent (more so in conservative allocations; less so in aggressive ones).

Many stock screens let you select small- and mid-size core stocks. I only consider core stocks that are large or very large because those companies have the greatest stability and endurance. Going smaller in core stocks doesn't make much sense to me.

Diversification and Stocks

In addition to considering the size and type of stock (core, growth, value), you need to be certain that stocks you add to your holdings are diversified. To the extent possible, diversification ensures that the same economic forces do not affect all your stocks. For example, high interest rates hurt makers of big-ticket items such as cars and housing by making financing more expensive. On the other hand, utilities and consumer staples (think toilet paper) do not drop as far as other stocks during an economic downturn—they also do not rise as fast or as far when the economy is booming. These stocks are called noncyclical or defensive because they help smooth out the peaks and valleys of the market (Chapter 5).

Dividend Reinvestment

Before we start looking at portfolio models, there's an important strategy that, over time, will provide a big boost to your return. Stocks that pay dividends are attractive investment targets. The dividends add to the stock's value by paying a quarterly dividend based on the number of shares you own. Dividends are reported in per-share amounts, so an annual dividend of $1 per share pays out in four payments of $0.25 per share.

You can take that cash and put it in the bank or whatever. However, if you don't have an immediate need for the cash, a better option is to reinvest it in the company's stock. If you sign up for a dividend reinvestment plan, your dividends buy more shares of the company's stock. Over time, this adds to your holdings and is a great way to up your return. Not every stock pays dividends or offers this option. If it's available, strongly consider signing up. Not all programs are the same, so make sure you understand the details. Also, note that even if you don't receive the dividends in cash, you may still be liable for the tax (Chapter 7).

Portfolio Models

Following are three models of portfolios that illustrate the range of asset allocation possibilities. Although they range from aggressive to conservative, there is not a point where investors switch from one to another. The transition is more like a sliding scale that begins with aggressive and is modified over time as it moves toward conservative. It is important to note that you do not have to start with an aggressive portfolio. I am assuming the aggressive portfolio is for young investors who are moving through their lives and modifying as they age. Many investors don't become serious about investing until they are older and more established (and have investment capital). If that fits you and you want to start very aggressively, that's fine as long as you fully understand the risks. On the other hand, if you are 25 years old and are only comfortable with a conservative approach, that's fine also. Where you start is up to you.

The following three portfolios simply illustrate possibilities. I used real stocks in these models but chose not to name them. I don't want to suggest any specific investment but rather illustrate the concept. These examples are just that: suggestions to illustrate my point. You must decide what works best for your financial needs, available investment capital, and risk tolerance. The examples depict portfolios in progress, not the starting point. Many beginning investors lack the available investment capital to acquire the completed portfolio. That's fine. The point is to get started and have a plan for completion.

Include Retirement Accounts

Remember to include any existing investments such as 401(k) or pension plans at work and any individual retirement accounts. They all count toward your completed portfolio. However, for this to work, you need to understand exactly where that money is invested. Most 401(k) and pension plans invest in funds managed by professionals. These funds are essentially mutual funds and offer a variety of options. You may not be able to change the options in a pension plan, but you can learn how it invests. If your retirement funds offer a choice that represents large-cap stocks, this can serve as your core holdings in the portfolio, leaving your private capital available to satisfy the other requirements. The same is true for foreign stocks, bonds, and other categories. You decide what works best.

The sum of your retirement accounts and your private investments represents your total invested capital. Apply the percentages in the sample portfolios or those you decide work best to that sum.

An Aggressive Portfolio

An aggressive portfolio attempts to significantly beat the market. To have a chance, you need a portfolio that is sufficiently aggressive to give you a chance, but you don't want it to be so far out that it is very risky. The important point to remember about risk and reward is that the reward part is only possible, not guaranteed. You stand to earn a high return or face a significant loss. I would say people who are 25 to 40 years old fit this portfolio, with people drifting into the moderate portfolio as they near 40.

Here's how an aggressive portfolio might look. (Percentages are of your total invested capital.)

- Stocks—80 percent
- Bonds—10 percent
- Cash—10 percent

Within the stocks component, an investor could consider a mix of something like this:

- Small-cap tech/growth stocks—25 percent
- Core holdings—30 percent
- Foreign stocks—15 percent
- Mid-cap growth stocks—30 percent

Small-cap tech/growth stocks example. At the time I created this, my choice was a small tech/growth firm that provides software and services for the healthcare industry, specifically electronic healthcare records for smaller clinics, hospitals, and practices. The company faces bigger and better-known competitors, so the risks are high. However, it could see dramatic increases if the company hits a sweet spot with smaller healthcare providers looking for a less expensive and simpler solution.

Core holdings example. The core holding is a household name, but many investors would be surprised to learn that most of its revenue comes from outside the United States. Its growth potential is in exploding markets such as China and India. Core holdings in an aggressive portfolio can have a sharper edge (more growth potential with slightly higher risk). This company will not grow as fast as predicted if global economic growth slows.

Foreign stock example. Foreign stocks are difficult to evaluate without a good service such as Morningstar. Their premium stock screener can be set for foreign stocks, although they must have a presence in the United States. Not surprisingly, many of the top-rated foreign stocks are involved with energy production and distribution. One Canadian example has large reserves tied up for exploration, and the future for continued high energy costs is good.

Mid-cap growth stock example. For this example, I chose a company in the video gaming industry. It is considered a market leader and is growing but hasn't had a recent blockbuster hit. Investors are concerned that it is no longer competitive in a very tough market. However, with a new hit title, the stock could soar.

While it is tempting to go "all in" with technology stocks in an aggressive portfolio, doing so subjects you to additional risks that the whole sector and all your stocks could crater. There are good growth opportunities outside technology.

A Moderate Portfolio

A moderate portfolio should target some stabilization in volatility; in other words, turn down the aggressive tactics in favor of a more moderate but more probably return. You still need growth to keep up and stay ahead of inflation and to push your return past the market's return. Bonds begin to play a larger role in the portfolio to add some stability. The moderate portfolio includes a larger presence for core stocks and a reduction in highly volatile small-cap issues. An age range for this portfolio might run from 40 to 55 years old. I have included only one stock for each example, although it is reasonable to assume that you may have the resources to own more than one stock per category at this stage in life. Because most investors add to their holdings over a period, it is also reasonable that your percentages will be different from these (you may want to use different percentages when you are comfortable with your understanding of the selection process).

Here's how a moderate portfolio might look (percentages are of your total invested capital):

- Stocks—60 percent
- Bonds—30 percent
- Cash—10 percent

Within the stocks component, an investor could consider a mix of something like this:

- Large growth stocks—25 percent
- Core holdings—45 percent
- Foreign stocks—10 percent
- Mid-cap value stocks—20 percent

Large growth stock example. The company I chose is dominant in the oil and gas service business with clients worldwide. Energy isn't getting any easier to find or recover, and this company will make money regardless of whether the resource is oil or gas and regardless of where the exploration is happening. No competitor is likely to capture much if any of its market share (very wide moat). A shift away from fossil fuels darkens the horizon, but even if that shift happens globally, it will be years before the company suffers dramatically.

Core holdings example. Another household name, this company offers a very diversified business with product lines in dozens of markets. They are a market leader in many industrial sectors where they compete, giving them a balance that helps prevent peaks and valleys in price and returns. Note: This example is a cyclical company; it would be prudent to add a noncyclical stock to the core holdings.

Foreign stock example. I would stay with the same company I picked in the aggressive portfolio, but I would reduce its presence. Other foreign stocks would also work as long as they were in politically stable economies like our previous Canadian example. Many 401(k) plans offer a foreign stock component, and that is an easy way to fill this portion of your portfolio.

Mid-cap value stock example. This example is a nationwide homebuilder with activity in multiple markets. The housing shortage is driving this business, along with other homebuilders. Shifting demographics and a severe housing shortage ensure a demand that will not be satisfied anytime soon. Although many competitors swim in the same waters, demand is such that supply will not catch up for years. Dragging-on growth, supply chain problems, rising interest rates, local regulations, and affordability issues challenge the whole industry. Successful participants need strict cost controls and ancillary services such as offering in-house financing to succeed. This company has sufficient tools to be a winner. A focus on entry-level homes and quality product make this consumer cyclical stock a good long-term prospect.

A Conservative Portfolio

A conservative portfolio is primarily focused on capital preservation, which means reducing the exposure to the volatility of stocks and locking in more principal in high-quality bonds and cash instruments. Thanks to healthcare advances, people are living longer, which means you must continue to risk some exposure to the stock market as a way to replenish the investment capital needed to convert to cash for living expenses. Persons age 55 and up should begin transitioning into this portfolio no later than age 55 and be out of aggressive holdings completely by around age 60—sooner or later, depending on your risk tolerance.

Here's how a conservative portfolio might look (percentages are of your total invested capital):

- Stocks—30 percent
- Bonds—50 percent
- Cash—20 percent

Within the stocks component, an investor could consider a mix of something like this:

- Core holdings noncyclical or defensive—55 percent
- Core holdings cyclical—45 percent

Core holdings noncyclical or defensive example. I broke core holdings up into noncyclical and cyclical issues. For this example, I picked a large healthcare company that makes a variety of name-brand and generic pharmaceuticals and over-the-counter products. Like most core holdings, it pays a strong dividend.

Core holdings cyclical example. I will use the previous example in the moderate portfolio. Because it is slightly more prone to growth, it may help keep the portfolio above water if inflation returns.

Rebalancing Your Portfolio

As you build your portfolio, maintain the correct percentages of your selections by rebalancing it at least once per year. The need to rebalance happens as your selections move up or down with the market. Gains or losses change the percentages of each area, and rebalancing brings them back into alignment.

To keep the math simple for this example, let's assume you have $100 in total invested (ignore rounding errors). You have chosen 50 percent stock, 30 percent bonds, and 20 percent cash. Your portfolio looks like this:

Stocks - $50 or 50%

Bonds – $30 or 30%

Cash - $20 or 20%

Total - $100 or 100%

Thanks to your excellent choices, one year later, your portfolio looks like this:

Stocks - $75 or 58%

Bonds - $35 or 27%

Cash - $20 or 15%

Total - $130 or 100%

Your portfolio is now worth $130. Good for you! However, the percentages are now off. Remember, you chose these percentages for a reason – growth, stability, and so on.

If you apply the balances to the portfolio goals, the distribution looks like this:

Stocks - $65 or 50%

Bonds - $39 or 30%

Cash - $26 or 20%

Total - $130 or 100%

Rebalance the portfolio by taking $10 out of stocks and distributing it between bonds and cash to hit your percentages. This is challenging since it may be counterintuitive to sell stocks when they have performed well, but the strategy (percentages) is more important. Look at all of your holdings, including retirement accounts, to make the adjustments. This also works when the market is against you and one area's percentage dips below where it should be. Move your capital around to rebalance the portfolio. This simple example only considers the three broad classes, but in practice, you also need to rebalance the components of each class. In particular, look at your stocks and make adjustments there also.

Pick a time each year for review and rebalance, such as after the first of the year when annual statements are available. If one area experiences a dramatic increase or decrease during the year, rebalance sooner if needed. Don't worry about changes of a few percentage points. Your portfolio percentages change as the market goes through its daily gyrations.

Portfolio Lessons

The example portfolios are purely illustrations and subject to your own financial situation and tolerance for risk. I will say that the general philosophy of moving from aggressive to conservative as you grow older is one you should adopt. History tells us that the stock market can be extremely volatile in the short run and that it can be a disaster for a person near or in retirement if substantial portions of their assets are in stocks. To make these (or any portfolio for that matter) work, you will also need to understand bonds, but that's another book.

Summary

Investing without a plan is like taking a road trip with no idea what state or town your destination is in. Your investing plan identifies your goal (retirement, for example), the vehicles you'll use (stocks, bonds, and cash), and your tolerance for risk (aggressive to conservative). Asset allocation spreads your capital among different investment options to reduce risk and aid growth. Stocks fall into broad categories representing degrees of risk and growth potential. The balance between risk and growth changes as you move from aggressive to conservative portfolios. This movement tracks the time remaining to reach the goal. Assigning percentages to each component of the portfolio represents your plan. At least once a year, rebalance your portfolio to the plan's percentages.

Chapter 9

Buying Stocks: DIY or Professional Help?

Now what?

You have a goal and a plan. You've figured out the right asset allocation and a comfortable level of risk. Your research has identified likely investment opportunities—none of which does any good until you actually begin investing.

The good news is you have many options. They range from completely do-it-yourself to engaging serious professional help. Take time to review the options below and see which one makes the most sense for you. Be honest with yourself. Going it alone can be challenging and requires work and continuing education. Using an investment professional makes sense for people with busy lives or who don't feel comfortable with the responsibility. The only correct choice is the one that works for you.

The following options represent broad descriptions of what is available. In many cases, job titles and services offered are at the discretion of the provider. The blurring of titles and services is common. Regulators require certain qualifications and licenses for investment professionals. Anyone providing investment advice and trading services must be licensed and follow certain regulations. These regulations do not require the provider to act in your best interest except in certain cases. Remember, they work for themselves, and while many do right by their clients, others put their interests ahead of those of their clients.

They may recommend products or services that pay a higher commission when a lower-priced alternative would suit the need.

Some investment professionals act as fiduciaries, which means they are legally bound to put your interests first. Generally, investment advisers act as fiduciaries, but this is not always true. As you will see, the lack of clear lines between titles and services confuses the question. Your best bet is to ask a provider up front or check their website.

How the Stock Market Works

Before I dig into the alternatives, a brief and very simplistic description of how the stock market works is in order. The "stock market" consists of different markets, many of which produce identical results. The New York Stock Exchange (NYSE) and the Nasdaq (Nasdaq, which originally stood for National Association of Securities Dealers Automated Quotations) are the two best-known markets. However, there are many other markets that take and process orders to buy or sell securities. Collectively, they are the stock market. If you want to get into the weeds, the internet has all the history and current status information you need.

The stock market can be thought of as an electronic auction. There are still a few humans involved in the process, such as at the NYSE, but a huge percentage of the process is totally automated. The stock market matches buyers and sellers. An order to buy shares of a stock is matched with a buyer willing to sell at a price agreed to by both. As I said earlier, the price is driven by supply and demand. More buyers than sellers means the price rises, and more sellers than buyers means the price falls. All of this happens in an instant. You offer to buy 100 shares of Acme Dynamite for $25 per share, and the market finds a buyer willing to sell at $25 per share. If there's no agreement, the market adjusts the price up or down until an agreement is reached. When an agreement is reached, you might not get the price you requested, though in many cases, the difference is pennies. There's a way to limit how much wiggle room in the price you'll accept, and I outline those later in this chapter. Unless your offer is way off, your order is filled in seconds.

The stock market is an ocean full of minnows and killer whales. You are a minnow. If you want to survive, do not attempt to compete with the killer whales. It won't end well for you. The minnows are the retail investors like you who trade for their own purposes. Individually, they have no impact on the market or prices because individual minnows are pursuing their own objectives and are not working as part of a school. When minnows do school, it's often to chase the hot new stock or sector (technology, for example), or they're fleeing in panic when things go south. A school of minnows is unflatteringly known in the business as "dumb money" or a buffet for the killer whales. A few minnows will escape with some of the prize, but most will not.

The killer whales are huge investment and trading machines that manage large sums of cash from pension funds, insurance companies, and other entities looking for a good return. They own most of the stock market and are collectively known as institutional investors. When they change their mind about a stock or sector, the stock market reacts.

Between the minnows and killer whales are a variety of different players, all of which also eat minnows. Some act like investors and look for a long-term return, but most are traders that may buy and sell hundreds of times a day on small price changes. They feed on minnows that unwisely believe they can compete with automated trading systems that make thousands of calculations per second.

Sounds grim, doesn't it? The truth is the stock market doesn't care when you buy a couple hundred shares of a stock. If you stick to your plan and avoid trading, the predators will never know you're there. That's why research is so important. If you know the fair market price, you'll know when to buy or sell.

Your Investing Options

How to execute your plan is a personal decision. There's no single "right way." Below is a general list of the alternatives. They range from doing everything yourself to handing over your cash and letting a professional make the decisions for you. These are not always well-defined roles. It's better to think of this as a continuum, with services bleeding between alternatives rather than strict definitions that fit all providers. Here are the alternatives:

- Full-service broker/financial adviser
- Discount broker
- Do-it-yourself/online broker
- Financial planner

The World of Stockbrokers

If nothing else, the world of stockbrokers is dynamic. What seems like just a few years ago, you could divide the pie into two basic pieces: full-service brokers and discount brokers. (Older readers may remember when there was only one type of stockbroker—one that was full-service with big commissions.) That changed when the industry was deregulated in 1975, opening commissions to market competition. This led to the advent of the discount broker. The growth of the internet really shook up the world of stockbrokers, giving investors the ability to perform brokerage services online.

While it is still not always easy to fit each broker into a neat pigeonhole, you can make a general distinction by the services they offer. Just remember that most firms have broadened their range of services to touch on almost all aspects of the stock market experience. You will also find specialty brokers who focus on particular market areas, such as options, bonds, or other more sophisticated investment products. I won't cover them in this book, but be aware that they are out there and always looking for new customers.

Full-Service Brokers

At the top of the service provider list are full-service brokers. Companies in this category offer a complete range of financial advisory services that extend beyond picking stocks to retirement planning and meeting other financial goals.

Some investors turn to full-service brokers for access to proprietary research on stocks and other financial instruments, along with the guidance of an investment professional. Many firms offer financial planning services that combine your investment accounts, retirement planning, and tax strategies. Full-service brokers maintain staffs that research and analyze stocks and bonds and offer proprietary analytical services that monitor your portfolio to minimize risk and maximize return.

Some full-service brokers also offer well-heeled investors the opportunity to participate in private offerings and provide access to hedge funds or other investments that are not generally available to the public. In many cases, to qualify for these services and products, you will need a significant six-figure pool of capital for investment and a very strong personal financial statement.

If you are uncomfortable making decisions about which stocks to buy or sell and want an experienced professional to help you, a full-service broker may be worth the higher fees and commissions. The key to a successful relationship with a full-service broker is finding an individual you trust within the company. The best way to find such an individual is by asking around and taking referrals from people you trust. Plan to meet with several brokers before making a decision. Make sure the chemistry is right and that you are comfortable with their experience and professionalism.

A good broker will listen to your goals, ask questions to determine your level of risk, and suggest appropriate products for your financial situation, age, and goals. Industry ethics and rules prevent brokers from putting you in inappropriate investments for your financial situation. However, this doesn't mean it never happens.

Even at their most basic service level, full-service brokers can be expensive. Commissions are higher, and some full-service brokers prefer to work on a percentage of your invested assets as an annual fee. For this arrangement, they provide a menu of services. It is important that you have a complete understanding of what is included in all fees and commissions, so there's no misunderstanding later.

Full-service brokers may also offer proprietary products such as mutual funds. They have an incentive to recommend these products. Be sure you have a full disclosure of fees and other expenses, as well as their performance history.

The pros of full-service brokers:

Following are the pros of working with a full-service broker:

- Professional help building your portfolio
- Access to proprietary research and products
- Can look at your total financial picture, including retirement planning and tax strategies

The cons of full-service brokers:

Following are the pros of working with a full-service broker:

- High fees for services
- Compensation may encourage excessive trading

- May push proprietary products that are not the best choice for you

Discount Brokers

Today's discount broker has evolved into more than an order taker. A big slice of the market wants something more than an order taker but less handholding than is provided by a full-service broker. Many of these brokers offer investment advice, but don't provide the comprehensive planning you might get with a full-service broker. They may have excellent research resources available on their websites and robust online capabilities.

Discount brokers and their close cousins, online brokers, offer many of the same services, so choosing between the two may be based on other factors. Many of the leading discount brokers now offer a variety of services that were once the domain of full-service brokers. However, in many cases, they may not offer investment advice. While some discount brokers may offer you the opportunity to speak directly with a broker who can at least offer some opinions on your decision, this will come at a higher price than their normal trade fee.

Not all discount brokers are equal. Avoid shopping for the lowest commissions because a few dollars saved per trade is inconsequential. Poor order execution and invisible customer service is not worth a few bucks per trade. If you stick with well-known discount brokers, this is not likely to happen. In addition, many of the better-known discount brokers have offices around the country, where you can go to set up an account or place an order. Some discount brokers offer access to research, which may come from a third party and with a fee. This is not a bad alternative if you want more detailed information than is readily available for free over the internet.

As with all brokers, it is important that you thoroughly understand the fees and commissions and any extra costs over and above the regular fees. (There's more about this in the stock orders section later in this chapter.) This should all be clearly explained on the company's website, or if you visit in person, you should be given a complete list of fees and commissions. Be especially careful about minimum deposits or account balances the company may require. If your balance drops below this minimum, you might pay either a monthly service fee or higher charges on your trades.

It's a good idea to visit the discount broker's website and become familiar with how they do business online. In some cases, the discount broker's website may let you open a practice account, where you can buy and sell stocks using fake money to become familiar with the software and how it works. If not, most discount brokers offer tutorials and even lessons on investing that may be helpful.

Long-term investors are usually not very active accounts for discount brokerages. You may not qualify for any special deals on commissions because you make only a few trades per year. The difference of a few dollars per trade is inconsequential when you seldom use the service. More important is how easy it is to access your account and make an order.

Discount broker pros:

Following are the pros of working with a discount broker:

- May offer some of the same services as full-service brokers without higher fees
- Usually don't require a high initial deposit
- Can access your account in person, by phone, by smartphone app, or from your computer

Discount broker cons:

Following are the cons of working with a discount broker:

- May charge extra for all but basic services
- No fee breaks for infrequent traders
- Watch for minimum balance requirements

DIY/Online Brokers

As the name states, you're on your own. It's the simplest and least expensive way to buy and sell stocks. Open an online account, fill out some forms, fund your account, and you're set.

Online brokers offer many of the same services that discount brokers do, though, of course, without physical offices. Most of the transactions they process come through their website, which may have a variety of options for you to consider. For example, some online brokers offer third-party research or other investment tools, such as portfolio monitors and price alerts if those are important to you.

While some online brokers will process phone orders, that is not the preferred method of communication. If you are comfortable working online and dealing with services over the web, this may not be an issue. However, what happens if you lose your internet connection or you happen to be somewhere your smartphone doesn't have a signal, and you need to place an order with your online broker? Also, there have been times during heavy market activity when some online brokers have had difficulty keeping up with incoming volume, which may mean their website is unavailable, perhaps when you need it the most.

As a rule, online brokers may offer the best rates and faster service in processing your orders. However, you could also say the same thing about many discount brokers. Squeezing a few dollars off commissions is less important than is the confidence that your order will be accepted and executed in a timely and correct manner. Some people would much rather deal with an online service than another human. If that's you, an online broker or a discount broker may make perfect sense.

Online brokers interact with you through a "dashboard," which is a work space where you connect with the market for quotes, to place orders, do research, and so on. The interface should be easy to navigate with a minimum of self-training through tutorials. Most of the major online brokers have well-tuned dashboards that let you get from one task to the next quickly.

With online brokers, it is especially important that they have prompt and reliable customer service, whether you reach them over the phone or online. There's nothing worse than not knowing if your order has been accepted or not.

Online broker pros:

Following are the pros of working with an online broker:

- Usually have the lowest commissions
- Quick execution with no upselling of products
- May offer some online tools/research with service

Online broker cons:

Following are the cons of working with an online broker:

- Research, if offered, tends to be generic
- Problems if the website is unavailable
- Virtually no help or guidance

Financial Planner/Adviser

I've included financial planner in the section to offer some clarity regarding the term. Earlier, I warned you about the overlapping and blurring of titles and services. One of the services many brokerages offer is financial planning. It's important to note that anyone can call themself a financial planner, with or without any training. Life insurance companies, wealth managers, stock brokerages, bankers, and so on have a stake in helping you with a financial plan.

A well-qualified, ethical financial professional will make building and managing your portfolio much easier. If you decide to use a financial professional, focus more on their qualifications and potential conflicts rather than what title they claim.

Financial Adviser vs. Financial Planner

The terms financial adviser and financial planner further muddy the waters. Basically, anyone who provides money management and investment advice is a financial adviser, including financial planners. A financial planner provides holistic, long-term planning to achieve your financial goals. An adviser may provide similar services and offer financial products and services. As with all investment products, do your homework and thoroughly investigate anyone offering to manage your investments, regardless of what they call themselves.

Several professional groups certify financial planners and provide continuing education. Professional financial planners fall into two basic types: fee-only and fee/commissions. The first type charges a fee to prepare a detailed financial plan covering savings, investments, insurance, taxes, and so on. The execution is up to you.

Commission-compensated financial planners (advisers) earn money from the products and services they put you in and may charge a fee for a detailed plan, although it will be much less than a fee-only planner. Many financial planners fall into this category and work for one of the industries mentioned above. This is not to say they don't do a good job; just remember where they earn money.

The gold standard is the certified financial planner (CFP). Certified professionals must act as a fiduciary, putting the client's interest first, regardless of any interests held by the professional's employer. If you want an objective plan, go with a CFP professional. You can find more information at https://www.cfp.net/.

Which Broker Type Is Right for You?

Picking a broker shouldn't be about price alone. Be honest with yourself about how much help you need, and go with the broker who fills any gaps in your knowledge and experience. The clearest distinction between broker types is full service and every other type of broker. When you begin comparing discount brokers and online brokers, you may find it hard to tell the difference between the two. Indeed, you could conclude that slotting every broker into only one of these types is not practical or useful.

When you know what you want from your broker, visit different websites and see if there is a good fit. If you have access to a discount broker's physical office, make an appointment and visit with a representative. If you stay with one of the major brokerages, you can be comfortable that they will take care of your business promptly and ethically. If they don't, I have a process you can use to have your complaint heard. In most cases, a visit with a supervisor can clear up many problems. Brokers live by referrals of satisfied customers and go to great lengths to avoid bad word-of-mouth comments. Thanks to social media, those complaints can spread rapidly and widely.

Opening a Brokerage Account

Before you can begin trading stocks, you must open an account with your broker. Depending on what type of broker you choose, opening an account can range from a very personal to a very impersonal process. There are several different types of accounts that most brokers offer in addition to the level of service you receive from the different types of brokers. First, I go over how the two basic types of brokers set up accounts, and then I describe the different types of accounts.

Be prepared with your Social Security number, bank account information, and a form of photo identification to open any brokerage account. You may need to email documents to an online broker's main office before they will open an account.

Full-Service Broker Accounts

A full-service broker goes over your financial situation in some detail. They will want to know about any debts, cash in the bank, any stock or mutual funds you own, retirement plans, insurance, home ownership, kids, your income, and so forth.

They are required to gather this information before they can make recommendations to you regarding investments. In the business, it's called "knowing your customer." The broker faces severe consequences for providing inappropriate investment recommendations to someone because the broker did not do their homework. This is one of the services you buy with the commissions and fees you pay to a full-service broker— recommendations that are appropriate for your individual financial situation. Many investors consider it money well spent.

Discount/Online Broker Accounts

Discount online brokers generally offer no advice and make no recommendations; therefore, setting up accounts with them is far less personal. There are still forms to fill out and questions to answer, but no one is going to come to your house and look at your checkbook. You are on your own in determining if the stock is right for you. Some particular types of investment (options, futures, and other high-risk investments) require you to certify that you are a knowledgeable investor and understand the risks associated with the product.

However, regulators are very particular about what might constitute a "recommendation" to buy or sell. If a broker in any way suggests, hints, or recommends a customer buy or sell a particular security, that constitutes a recommendation and the broker must have the necessary "know your customer" forms on file and be registered as an investment adviser. If an online or discount broker provides you with access to research but doesn't suggest a particular security—and you have the ability to research any security you want—that does not qualify as a recommendation.

Types of Accounts

There are several types of accounts that most brokers offer. They include:

- Cash accounts
- Margin accounts
- Discretionary accounts

There may be others that are particular to individual brokerages, but they are variations of one of these three types.

Cash Accounts

A cash account is the simplest type of brokerage account and the first one you will probably open. Online and discount brokers will most likely require you to make a deposit with enough money to cover your trade before opening your account. Many will place this money in an interest-bearing account until you are ready to trade. When you place a buy order, the broker transfers the money to the brokerage account to cover the trade. When you sell a stock, the broker will deposit the proceeds in the account (unless you instruct them otherwise), so cash is available for the next purchase. Be sure you understand the policy of the broker you choose.

Margin Accounts

Margin accounts allow you to borrow money from the broker to buy stocks. A margin account allows you to borrow up to 50 percent of the value of the stock from your broker when you make a purchase. For example, if you want to buy $10,000 of stock, you could pay with money in your account. With a margin account, transfer $5,000 from your account and borrow $5,000 from your broker. Obviously, these accounts require more documentation and a stellar credit rating, and not all stocks qualify for margin trading.

By borrowing one-half the value of the stock, you can multiply your profits dramatically. Here's how that works: If the stock price doubles to $20,000, your investment in the margin account ($5,000) increases four-fold. You sell the stock and pay back the $5,000 you borrowed from the broker. Your $5,000 has earned $10,000. If you paid cash for the stock ($10,000), you would have earned the same $10,000, but on a $10,000 investment. That's a dramatic difference in return on your investment.

With a margin account, you can make your money work harder. However, there is risk. Suppose the stock falls to $5,000. You pay back the $5,000 you borrowed from the broker, and you're left with a total loss. If you had paid cash, you would have $5,000 left instead of nothing. These are extreme examples to illustrate the benefits and dangers of margin trading.

If the value of the stock falls instead of rises, your broker will issue a "margin call" when there's not enough money in your investment account to cover the loan. However, some brokers may have different thresholds for margin calls. This threshold is called the margin maintenance requirement. When you get a margin call, you have two options: You can deposit cash into the account to raise the value above the amount you borrowed, or you can sell the stock immediately and pay off the loan. Some brokers may not give you the option of depositing cash; they may liquidate your position for you when the stock falls below a certain price. Because this is a loan from your broker, expect to pay interest on the borrowed amount.

Trading on margin has appeal, and when it works in your favor, it's a wise move. However, don't get excited with the prospect of "easy money." Speculation is a game you will lose.

Discretionary Accounts

Discretionary accounts give a broker or financial adviser the right to buy and sell stock without notifying you. If a broker wants this authorization, go find another broker. Unless you trust a broker or financial adviser with your life, never give anyone this type of control over your finances—it is the equivalent of a blank check. There are circumstances when these types of accounts are appropriate; however, for most of us, they are inappropriate.

Stock Market Orders You Should Know

The world of buying and selling stocks has its own language, which may sound confusing, but fortunately, long-term investors need only master a few of the basic orders. You will communicate your orders to your broker by whatever method is appropriate. The orders are industry standard, and there shouldn't be much variation among different brokers. It is important that you know what happens when each type of order is executed, so there will be no unpleasant surprises.

The basic orders are to buy or sell, though it is a bit more complicated than that. You need to specify what type of buy or sell order you want. Here are the stock market orders you need to know.

Market Orders

The order is the simplest and quickest way to get your order filled (or completed). A market order instructs your broker to buy or sell the stock immediately at the prevailing price, whatever that may be. Unless you tell your broker, the order is processed as a market order. For highly traded, large-cap stocks, this is usually a safe order. Otherwise, you may not get the price you want with a market order. This is a dangerous order if you're concerned about buying or selling at a certain price (and you should be).

Limit Orders

Limit orders instruct your broker to buy or sell a stock at a particular price. The purchase or sale will not happen unless you get your price. Limit orders give you control over your entry or exit point by fixing the price, which can be helpful. Limit orders are your best choice in most cases, especially for smaller or less-traded stocks. For example, if you decide you want to buy Stock A at no more than $25 per share and it is currently trading at $27 per share, you could put a limit buy order in for $25 per share. If the stock drops to that point, your order will be executed. Note that if the price drops below your price, you may still pay the $25 per share because the market takes the best orders first. The same process works for limit sell orders. If you will sell at a price above or below the current market price (to protect a profit or cut a loss), a limit buy order is appropriate (see stop-loss orders next).

Stop-Loss Orders

A stop-loss order gives your broker a price trigger that protects you from a big drop in a stock. You enter a stop-loss order at a point below the current market price. If the stock falls to this price point, your broker sells the stock. If the stock stays level or rises, the stop-loss order does nothing. Stop-loss orders are cheap insurance that protects you from a loss.

Trailing Stops

The trailing stop order is similar to the stop-loss order, but you use it to protect a profit, as opposed to protecting against a loss. You can use the trailing stop order to follow the stock price as it goes up. You enter the trailing stop order as a percentage of the market price. If the stock continues to rise, the trailing stop follows it up because it is a percentage of the market price. This protects your additional gains. If the market price declines by that percentage, your broker sells the stock. For long-term investors, trailing stops are for stocks you want to sell after allowing them rise in price as long as possible. When the price retreats, the trailing stop kicks in, and you are out of the stock with your profit.

Placing an Order with Your Broker

A limit order, whether given to a stockbroker or entered into an online system, has the same five components:

- Buy or sell
- Number of shares
- Security
- Order type
- Price

For example, if you wanted to buy 100 shares of XYZ using a limit order, here's how you would express it:

Buy 100 shares of XYZ: limit 33.45

This order tells the market you will buy 100 shares of XYZ, but under no circumstances will you pay more than $33.45 per share.

It will take some experience to know where to set limit orders. If you set limit buy orders too low, they may never be filled, which does you no good. The same is true for limit sell orders. With some experience, you'll find the spot that gets you a good price and your order filled.

How to Keep Investing Expenses Low

The expenses of investing in the stock market can cut into your returns if you are not careful. I already discussed taxes in Chapter 7, which are a major expense if you do not properly time your transactions. Another obvious expense is the cost of doing business with a broker. There are commissions, fees, and other costs (such as extra fees for limit orders). Beyond that, you can rack up plenty of extra expenses that may pay for services or products you don't need. Here are some of the more common expenses:

Research and analysis. There are hundreds of research services on the web that range from free to inexpensive to outrageous. I have already noted that the premium features of Morningstar are worth the modest fee. Other offerings may cost hundreds of dollars per month. Some are delivered via email, while others come from in-person seminars, often at lavish resorts. Be very careful about what you pay for investment research and analysis.

Investing or trading systems. Every day, at least it seems that way, someone else comes up with a "revolutionary" system that promises triple-digit returns and all types of unbelievable success if you just use their simple system. Not likely.

Hardware/software. You do not need expensive hardware (computers) or software to be successful as a long-term investor. Any relatively new computer will be perfectly adequate, and the software you need is available from your broker over the web. Online providers assume you have a broadband (high-speed) internet connection.

Publications/newsletters. There are some good paid subscription publications and newsletters for interested investors. Whether you are considering a paid or free publication, be sure you understand what, if anything, the publisher has to gain. (Do they sell financial products, and does the content direct you toward a purchase?)

A popular ploy is to offer a seminar on investing at a luxury resort and suggest that you can write off the cost as an investment expense. Never take tax advice from someone who has something to gain if you follow the advice.

What You Do When Things Go Badly

As an investor, you have certain rights that your broker must acknowledge. As previously noted, brokers have a legal and ethical responsibility to deal with you fairly and appropriately. Unfortunately, like any business, brokers sometimes bend or break the rules. Bad actors (large and small) are out there, so investors beware.

Despite the unfortunate headlines, the securities industry is one of the most highly regulated businesses in the United States. The U.S. Congress is at the top of the heap. It created most of the structure, and it passes major laws that affect how the industry operates. It also authorizes budgets for the Securities and Exchange Commission (SEC) and other agencies involved in regulatory duties. The SEC is the top regulatory agency responsible for overseeing the securities industry. It registers new securities and handles all the filings that public companies must make, such as annual and quarterly reports.

The SEC

The SEC also oversees all stock exchanges and any organization connected with the selling of securities. It also has a strong anti-fraud unit that monitors advertising and marketing to make sure companies comply with strict rules concerning the sale of securities. You can find all of the public filings (financial statements and so on) on the SEC's website.

Financial Industry Regulatory Authority (FINRA)

At the next level is the Financial Industry Regulatory Authority (FINRA). It was created in 2007 when the National Association of Securities Dealers merged with the regulatory functions of the New York Stock Exchange. It is an industry self-regulatory body that is responsible for policing the securities industry. FINRA sets standards for stockbrokers and other industry professionals and licenses them after comprehensive examinations.

FINRA has the ability to fine individuals and organizations for unethical behavior and can revoke licenses. Usually, FINRA is the place customers can take complaints about behavior they feel is unethical or illegal. FINRA also monitors the trading activities of member firms to detect illegal patterns and other questionable activity. The individual exchanges also have sophisticated regulatory oversight functions within their own operations. These include monitoring trades and other steps to see that the customer gets a fair deal. Search for FINRA on the web for the nearest office and how to file a complaint.

Individual States

Individual states also have securities divisions, although they are usually not as sophisticated as FINRA. They often handle complaints and register securities that will be sold within the state's boundaries, although this will vary from state to state. You can find contact information for your state's security regulation departments at http://www.nasaa.org/about-us/contact-us/contact-your-regulator/.

Broker's In-House Monitoring

The final step of protection (or the first in order of where you should start) is at the brokerage level. Each firm is required to keep certain records and perform certain checks and audits of the operation to make sure their brokers are operating within acceptable legal and ethical guidelines. If you have a problem, contact the managing broker. Many problems can be solved at this level.

Please note that losing money on a trade, even one an adviser recommended, is usually not grounds for a complaint.

Summary

Deciding on how much help you want or need is the beginning of your search for a stockbroker. While it's possible to assign the various alternatives to broad categories, it's best to focus more on what the firm offers. A full-service broker offers a variety of products and services for a price, but if you need or want this type of help it's worth the cost. Discount and online brokers provide some of the same services, but they take a more hands-off posture. A general knowledge of account types and market orders prepares you to begin buying and selling stocks. Financial planners/advisers provide various levels of help managing your money. When things go south, you have a number of steps to correct problems and solve disputes.

Chapter 10

Avoiding Mistakes, Traps, and Schemes

One of the best ways to make money in the stock market is to avoid losing it. No one wants to lose money, but the reality of investing dictates loss is likely. There is no foolproof way to only pick winners. Investors can, however, avoid costly common mistakes, traps, and schemes. Investors create their own problems by failing to act, acting emotionally, or ignoring the facts.

Any task is easier if you have the right tools, and investing is no different. Thankfully, most of the tools are easy to access and help simplify the process and mechanics of investing. However, tools do you no good if you don't use them. Base decisions on facts and analysis.

Common Investing Mistakes and How to Avoid Them

We all make mistakes, but there are some that we can avoid if we know what they are beforehand. Investing in stocks, like anything involving money, is an emotion-laden experience. For some investors, it is easy to put their anxieties aside and focus on the facts. For others, money is more complicated, and dodging the emotional minefields is more difficult. Where you fall on this spectrum may make it easier or harder to avoid mistakes. Even investors with difficult relations with money can avoid mistakes if they see them coming. The following mistakes can trip up anyone, so be forewarned.

Playing Catch-Up

One of the most common problems investors face is trying to catch up for the years they missed contributing to a retirement plan. With millions of baby boomers approaching retirement, panic has set in among those who have not adequately planned for how they will fund their retirement. In some cases, pensions were wiped out when companies went bankrupt, people were unemployed for significant periods of time, or they generally just did not think far enough ahead to put money away for retirement.

As middle age approaches, they panic because of all the years they missed investing in their retirement. Instead of investing, they chose to do something else with their money or simply did not have the money to spare. A common solution is an aggressive approach in hopes of picking winning stocks that will make up for 20 years of inactivity.

The problem here, of course, is that making excessively risky bets in the stock market almost always ends poorly. High-risk investments mean that many, if not all of them, will fail to achieve expected results and may, in fact, come crashing down.

You can't make up for decades of inactivity by becoming hyperactive in middle age or later. So, what is a middle-aged person to do when they realize they have few, if any, assets put away for retirement? In most cases, their best bet is to follow a commonsense strategy to build the retirement fund as rapidly and responsibly as they can. Here are some steps they can take:

Review your budget. Take a hard look at your budget and begin cutting as many luxuries as you can out of your monthly spending:

- Don't buy a new car every couple of years.
- Drop expensive club memberships if you use them infrequently.
- Skip the vacation to Europe and stay closer to home.
- Do you really need all those streaming services?

Review other steps you can take to save money in other ways, and add those extra dollars to your retirement account.

Retirement plan. If you work for an employer with a retirement plan, such as a 401(k), increase your participation by as much as possible. There are limits on how much you can contribute, and your human resources department can explain those to you.

Additional cash. Any additional cash you can find should go into an appropriate investment model portfolio that is based on your financial situation and time remaining to retirement. Rather than investing in high-risk stocks, keep your investments in line with what's appropriate for your age. At this point, you cannot afford to take losses on risky investments.

Fall in Love with a Stock or a Company

I am a big fan of Apple products. For me, they provide an extremely functional experience with style and sophistication. I wish I had spent as much time analyzing Apple stock as I did following its products. The stock was dirt-cheap in the early 2000s compared to 20-plus years later. As it turned out, Apple would have been a great buy; however, buying Apple stock because I loved its products would have been a gamble, not a sound investment decision. In this case, the gamble would have paid off handsomely. Does anyone remember VHS tapes or audiocassette tapes? I have boxes of both sitting in my basement. I loved those, too and I'm glad I didn't invest in them either. There's nothing wrong with investing in a company you love, just be sure to you've objectively concluded it's also a great investment also.

It is too bad that I didn't invest in Apple stock, but it points out a mistake that many people make. If I decide to buy Apple stock, it will be based on my research that indicates it still has room to climb, and I can buy it at a reasonable price. It will not be based on the fact that I'm a big fan of their products.

It seems like every week, there is a new stock market darling. Investors who buy the stock based on the excitement factor may have a rude awakening when the company's fundamentals don't live up to its image. This is not to say that a popular company can't also be a good investment. The key is to look for financial strength. A wide economic moat and all of the other factors that make a great company are discussed in earlier chapters.

Years ago, a company named Enron was a media darling, and its high-flying stock charmed the investing public. Many investors didn't understand exactly how they made their money. Company executives encouraged employees to put their 401(k) contributions into Enron stock. When it came to light that company officials were manipulating the financial information they reported to stockholders and the SEC, the company stock went into a nosedive. In the end, the company was bankrupt, and stockholders lost everything. The real tragedy was that the company's employees, who had no idea of the fraud, had most of their retirement savings wiped out when the stock became worthless.

The mistake here is not looking at every company you are considering investing in through the same logical process regardless of how much you like the company or how much the media and investment community loves the company.

The second lesson is to never put a large chunk of your assets in one company. A good public relations campaign is no substitute for a financially healthy and well-run company. Great companies demonstrate their worth in their financial statements, economic moat, and the other factors used to analyze its health.

The investment landscape is littered with companies that have had their moment in the sun but failed at a fundamental business level or that were tied to an industry or consumer segment that was not growing or was saturated with competitors.

A few companies fail due to fraud. Most fail because management does not adapt to changing markets and business realities. Fax machines were once the rage. Now, most have been replaced by email and other online communication options.

Market Timing

Market timing may be the two most dangerous words in investing. Timing the market is about buying a stock just before it begins a rapid move upward. Almost everyone who's been involved in the stock market at one time or another has seen opportunities they are convinced will make them a large sum of money because somehow they have predicted the future price of a stock or stock market indexes. After the fact, they can do what I did with Apple stock and say if only I had bought that stock on this date, I would be a rich person now. Of course, everyone is great at looking at the stock market through the rearview mirror and picking winners.

The mistake comes when investors convince themselves that they or someone else can predict a winner before it happens. It is called timing the market because investors convince themselves that if they buy now, it will just precede a huge increase that will make them rich. To set the record straight, there is no system, no software, no technique, and no crystal ball that will tell you with any consistency which way the market is moving. Yet, you will see dozens, if not hundreds, of systems, strategies, software, or whatever claiming to do exactly this. Many investors abandon their research and go with a hot tip or gut feeling. It is even possible that you may guess correctly once or twice; however, the 8 or 10 other times, you will guess wrong, and those losses will outweigh any gains you make on a correct guess.

Ask yourself: if you had a surefire system to beat the market every time, would you sell it for $99 or even $9,000? If I had such a system, why would I need to sell it to others, and wouldn't a large adoption diminish its effectiveness? Yet, there are dozens of such systems floating around the internet.

You should ask yourself: Do I want to bet my retirement or my kids' college education on a guess? The strategies I have outlined in this book are time-tested and proven: identify great companies, buy them at a great price, and hold on to them for the long term. This buy-and-hold strategy has its detractors, most of whom are convinced they have a system they would love to sell you. They claim that their market timing system pulls you out of the market before it collapses and gets you back in when it begins its ascent. They charge that buy-and-hold investors watch their account value drop along with the market when they could avoid those drops if they only used this system.

The best response to their allegations is to point to Warren Buffett, who is acknowledged as the most successful investor of all time. His investment strategy remained consistent throughout his career, and that was to buy great companies at great prices and let them build wealth over the years.

Abandoning Your Plan When the Market Drops

One of the classic mistakes investors make is to abandon their investment plan when the market goes into a deep dive. Ask any stockbroker what happens when the market takes a nosedive, and almost every one of them will tell you that their phone won't stop ringing from clients who want to cash out of the stock market.

As previously noted, money is a very emotional topic, and the fear of loss is the strongest emotion of all. It is difficult and painful to watch the value of your portfolio follow the market down into what may seem like a bottomless pit. The first reaction of many investors is to simply sell everything and take their money out of the stock market. That is almost always exactly the wrong thing to do. How should an investor react when the market is on one of its rollercoaster rides pointing down?

Under any circumstances, when you are making a decision, the first step is to re-examine the companies you own to verify they still fit into your overall investment plan. If something has fundamentally changed about the company—for example, they have lost their economic advantage or have become financially unstable—you should seriously consider selling the stock regardless of what the stock market is doing.

One of the few things we know for certain about the stock market is that it will go up, and it will go down. However, no one has a clear idea when either of these events is going to happen. The strategy I've outlined in this book will protect you as much as possible during those times when the stock market is going down, and it will create the opportunity for growth when the market is going up.

If you have a plan and stick to it, bumps in the market will not frighten you into poor decisions. Market rollercoasters come and go, such as the one that began in early 2020 when the impact of the COVID-19 pandemic suddenly stalled the economy. The S&P 500 Index, considered "the market" by professional investors, sat at about 3,380 in early February (the high for the year at that point). Investors saw the index plunge 25 percent in a few weeks. Yet, in the face of this disaster, the S&P 500 recovered not only the lost 25% but went on to set record highs. By the end of 2021, the index closed at about 4,766, an increase of some 107% from its 2020 low. Investors who panicked and fled the market in early 2020 missed out on tremendous gains. For investors, the best strategy after re-evaluating all of the companies and confirming they still meet the qualifications you needed when you bought them is to remain in the market and let your great companies do what they do best. When the market rebounds, you will be there with your great companies to participate in the recovery.

Remember, the daily stock market gyrations have nothing to do with the value a company creates. Over time, great companies create wealth through consistent profits and, in many cases, dividends.

Rules Have Changed

This mistake is sometimes known as "the rules are different this time." Like a lot of the stuff you hear about the stock market, the problem with this mistake is that it is never different this time or any time, and the important rules never change. Yet every time we see a bubble in the stock market, the know-it-alls tout the same tired and wrong pronouncements. During the dot-com boom, it was the "new economy" or the "web economy" that excited the market—the old rules didn't apply anymore. In March 2000, the NASDAQ Composite closed at just more than 5,000. That same month, the dot-com bubble burst. The NASDAQ bottomed out at 1,100—a staggering 78 percent loss.

In the early 2000s, real estate became the new "hot" topic. Housing prices soared, and large investment firms began selling securities backed by "subprime" mortgages, meaning the loan should never have been made. In the mid-2000s, the housing market crashed, with millions of defaulted loans causing a financial system crash that spread to a global contraction. Aggressive action by the government prevented a depression that would have crippled the economy. They couldn't avoid a severe recession, the largest in recent history.

Ultimately, the market always corrects to valuation. If a stock has the numbers and insightful management, it will continue a growth trend when able. Value investors count on the market correcting to value because when that happens, the underpriced stock they bought will take off.

Some Other Investing Mistakes

The following are some of the other classic mistakes investors make when they let their fear or greed overrule their plan:

Hot tips. Acting on hot tips is almost always a recipe for overpaying. By the time you hear about a "hot tip," the professional traders have bought and sold the stock and made their profit. You will buy at the top of an inflated price that will almost certainly fall well below what you paid.

Forgetting trading costs. It's easy to forget that it costs money now and in the future to make a profit on a stock trade. In the present, there is a commission to pay; in the future, you will pay a commission when you sell and taxes on any profits. Which taxes you pay will depend on how long you held the stock before you sold it. A stock's price must rise enough to cover all the past trading costs, future trading costs, and the anticipated taxes and still have a nice profit for you.

Poor asset allocation/diversification. If your asset allocation (Chapter 8) is not well defined, you're setting yourself up for a major setback. Diversification lowers your risk by spreading your investing dollars over industries and asset classes. As you build a portfolio, you may not have the resources to quickly achieve good diversification. In the interim, buy a low-cost market index mutual fund or exchange traded fund to help with diversification.

Inability to sell. Investors sometimes have a difficult time admitting to themselves that an investment isn't working out. They hold on irrationally, hoping the company is going to bounce back from the brink of bankruptcy. Investors should set a loss limit and sell when the stock hits that mark.

Giving up too soon. Investing in stocks is a long-term commitment—at least five years or more. Even companies with good fundamental economics may stall in price. If you had a logical reason for investing in the company in the first place, be patient and let the market catch up with your thinking.

Fads and Fakes and Frauds

Here is a truth of human nature: the allure of "easy money" is almost irresistible. Look no further than the millions who play some form of lottery each day, hoping for that big payoff. I'm not judging people who play responsibly, though a lotto ticket is not a retirement plan. I saw a saying somewhere that sums it up: Your chances of winning the lottery are only slightly improved if you buy a ticket.

Add gambling (legal and otherwise), and it's clear people are drawn to the prospect of easy money. Sure, visiting a casino or betting on the horses is great entertainment, but for many, it's so much more.

Investing is building wealth over time with acceptable levels of risk and expected returns. Yet, there's a whole industry dedicated to removing money from your pocket and putting it in theirs with can't-miss trading tips, "the next Apple!" and other schemes. Some are just misguided traders who believe they've discovered something no one else sees. Some were right once and now believe they have some special insight. Some are outright frauds who prey on the greedy or gullible.

And then there are the self-inflicted mistakes of jumping on the current hot trend because that's what is burning up social media or your friends' attention. It's human nature to join a group. If the group thinks investing in silver is smart, the temptation to belong makes poor decisions seem fine. Here are some examples:

Crowdsourcing through Social Media to Manipulate the Market. Some individuals believe they can encourage enough people to overpower large institutional investors by directing the purchase or sale of a security. While some may make money, most end up regretting their actions. Social media is a powerful voice and can sway large groups of people to take actions that defy logic in the name of "beating the system" that they argue is stacked against individuals. I don't disagree with the idea that the system is stacked against individuals; this is why I urge investors to avoid trying to beat it. As the casino operators learned a long time ago: the house always wins. Casinos and investing hustlers love to point out big winners; it just encourages more suckers to try their luck.

Never follow a crowd in chasing some system or idea that suggests it knows how to beat the system. Ask yourself this: Who starts these efforts, and what do they have to gain? It's not your success they work for.

Penny Stocks. This is one of the oldest investing traps. Penny stocks are usually small, often struggling companies whose stock is not listed on major markets. The stock often sells for a few dollars or less. In many cases, the companies are blameless victims used to con people out of their money. Some people honestly believe there are opportunities in penny stocks— think of them as the ultimate value stock. One big product or partnership can thrust the company into the big leagues, accompanying a huge rise in the stock's price. More often, penny stocks are used by crooks who tout some inside knowledge ("the next Microsoft") to encourage others to jump in. In reality, the crooks have already bought huge blocks of the stock at rock-bottom prices. If their promotion is successful, the stock's price skyrockets as naïve buyers jump in. When the promoters think they've pushed the price up as far as it will go, they sell their shares at the inflated price and walk away with the profits while the stock's price crashes. The company honestly professes not to understand the reason for the price swings.

In the industry, this is known as "pump and dump" and it has been around in some form for years. Never buy a penny stock. There's no legitimate reason to ever waste money that could go toward investing in a great company with real potential to build your wealth over time.

Cryptocurrency. Beginning in 2009, cryptocurrency, or cryptos, rose from relative obscurity to the hottest investing idea in decades. I won't attempt to explain how it works because

I don't understand the blockchain technology that makes cryptos possible, and I suspect many who are jumping on the bandwagon don't either. Cryptos are not stocks, but there are a growing number of ways to invest in the phenomenon. As noted earlier, the allure of easy money is almost irresistible. Here's what I do understand:

Cryptos are software. There's no physical asset underlying them, which is the whole point, apparently. Crypto value seems to be derived from scarcity and demand—in other words, supply and demand. For this and other reasons, most professionals either won't touch cryptos or take a wait-and-see attitude. Most avoid cryptos because there's no reliable way to place a value on them. Cryptos change hands in obscurity, which means transactions may not be visible to tax authorities or law enforcement. So, guess how some people use cryptos?

Is there a legitimate role for cryptos in our economy and investment portfolio? As of this writing, the jury is still out among financial professionals, although you wouldn't know that with all the hype, including Hollywood stars' endorsements. Here's a good rule: A great actor does not automatically make a great financial adviser. Remember to follow the money. Any person or organization that backs an investment idea (cryptos, stocks, or anything) often stands to gain from your participation. Do they have your best interests in mind? I always doubt that anyone cares about my financial well-being more than I do.

Ten years from now, I may write another book and include cryptos as a legitimate part of every investment portfolio. I may also figuratively pound my head for not investing in cryptos earlier. But I don't think so, and I'm sure not betting my retirement on something nobody can place an accurate valuation on.

The Biggest Trap

The largest danger to investing success is you. No one forces you to invest in wild tips, suspicious trading systems, or anything else. Stick with a logical, fact-based plan and ignore 99 percent of the noise from the market. You're unlikely to be right all of the time, but the mistakes will be honest ones. Learn from them and move on.

Not the End

This is not the end of your education; instead, it's the beginning. I've given you a broad outline of the process and directed you to expert resources for more information and help. Where you go from here is up to you. If you are prepared to do the work, investing in individual stocks can be rewarding and profitable. You may decide this is too much for a variety of reasons and decide to engage a qualified professional for help. That's fine. With this outline, you'll be a better client and understand what the professional recommends and why. If you want to go it alone but don't have the resources to engage a professional, read up on "index investing." This strategy substitutes low-cost index mutual funds for the individual stocks and bonds in my portfolio examples. A good stock fund and a quality bond fund are all you need.

No matter how you decide to proceed, please proceed, even in small increments. The longer you put off executing a retirement plan, the harder it will be to reach your goal.

Shameless self-promotion: I have a website at investingforboomers. com that provide more information on retirement investing, especially for folks in the baby boomer generation. Also, my books are available at Amazon.com.

Good luck!

Summary

Where money is involved, always expect that someone covets yours and has a plan to get it. It sounds harsh, but if you aren't careful, bad things are likely to happen. Sometimes, we self-inflict problems with common investing mistakes such as trading instead of investing or letting your emotions override our reasoning. Money attracts bad actors who have numerous ways to scam you. No one has a secret strategy that guarantees winning trades, but they will fatten their wallets with the fees you pay. Some products are toxic to your wealth, such as penny stocks and cryptocurrency schemes. The cliché says if it seems too good to be true, it's probably because it isn't. Apply that to your investing and every other money decision you make.

Index